# GETTING THERE

# GETTING THERE
# A BOOK OF MENTORS

BY GILLIAN ZOE SEGAL ABRAMS IMAGE, NEW YORK

FOR SAGE

# TABLE OF CONTENTS

# INTRODUCTION

I used to imagine that highly successful people were practically born that way—that they either had a meteoric rise to the top or, at the very least, enjoyed a smooth, steady climb along some primrose path. Although I grew to realize that this is not true, I was still continually taken aback by the singular stories the subjects of this book told me—the obstacles they overcame, the setbacks they endured, and the defining moments (sometimes even in childhood) that infused them with the tenacity and strength they needed to prevail.

I thought about how this book would help everyone from students just starting to contemplate their futures to those well into a successful career—and especially my daughter, Sage. I couldn't wait to incorporate the lessons my subjects imparted into my parenting, and hoped that one day Sage would be happy to have this compendium of wisdom at her fingertips—a series of unguarded, intimate pep talks from some of the world's most influential and inspirational figures.

It wasn't until I was halfway through the project, however, that I understood what was truly motivating me. They say that people teach what they need to learn. While I am genuinely excited to inspire my daughter and others, I believe I was drawn to create this book because *I* desired guidance and inspiration from these luminaries.

My own career trajectory began with a plan to follow an explicit, linear path that culminated at a distinct destination—but as I entered my early twenties, the path became quite circuitous.

Like most parents, mine wanted my three brothers and me to grow up to be successful. And in our household, success was pretty much defined by two things: wealth and being your own boss. Since a career was viewed as a means to financial autonomy, we were discouraged from pursuing things we enjoyed but that were unlikely to lead to a large income. Instead, we were urged to go to law school (it's good training for anything), then immediately, embark upon a financially motivated entrepreneurial venture. I reasoned that, while it was certainly quite specific, this wasn't a *bad* plan. After all, who wouldn't want to be rich and independent?

During law school, I contemplated different ways to make my fortune but nothing either drew me in or seemed like the right fit. As graduation neared, I became increasingly anxious about what I would do afterward. I started to wonder if I was going about planning my future the right way, and I spent a lot of time trying to figure out how others had discovered their callings and forged their paths.

A real turning point occurred when, shortly after taking the bar exam, I read a commencement address given by the cartoonist Cathy Guisewite at my alma mater, the University of Michigan. Cathy spoke about the moment she realized she wanted to write for a living and suggested that, when deciding what to do with the rest of their lives, the graduates remember what they love: *"Take the classes, the friends, and the family that have inspired the most in you. Save them in your permanent memory and make a backup disk. When you remember what you love, you will remember who you are. If you remember who you are, you can do anything."*

Cathy's words resonated with me. Following her advice, I thought back over my four years at Michigan. I had been most energized by the photography course I took the last semester of my senior year. Drawn immediately to portraiture, I found joy in connecting with different types of people and would spend hours in the darkroom studying and developing prints. I decided to pursue this interest and enrolled in a one-year program at the International Center of Photography (ICP). Soon after that, I hatched the idea for my first book, *New York Characters*.

The theory behind *New York Characters* is that what makes New York such an amazing city is its people. Among the millions of New Yorkers, there are some who become famous in their own subcultures and give the Big Apple its flavor. I began photographing and interviewing them. My subjects included neighborhood fixtures, prominent celebrities, and the truly eccentric.

Working on *New York Characters* was a dream come true. Every day felt like an adventure as I discovered different pockets of my city and got to know a broad cross section of its population. However, getting a book published when I had no track record as a photographer or writer didn't prove to be an easy task.

Beginning with the traditional route, I put together a book proposal and shopped around for an agent. *No one* wanted to represent me. When I approached teachers at ICP for advice, they told me that I should start by interning for an established photographer, then work on my own résumé, *then* try to get a book published. Ignoring this advice, I decided to take the bull by the horns and represent myself. I parked myself in a bookstore, combed through the photography and New York sections, and made a list of the publishers that might be interested in a book like mine. I even read the acknowledgment sections of certain books so I knew the specific person to target at each company. To make a long story short, the first publisher I contacted, W. W. Norton & Company, loved my work and ended up publishing *New York Characters*.

But even with a contract from a well-known publisher, I had a difficult time getting subjects to participate in my book. My rule became that until I received a definite no from a subject I would continue to politely contact him or her until my deadline arrived. (Who am I kidding? Even when I did get a definite no, I wasn't deterred. I would wait a bit then look for another angle from which to approach.) I called Spike Lee's office at least thirty times, befriended one of his assistants over the phone, and had him go to bat for me. If I hadn't been so passionate about *New York Characters,* I wouldn't have had the resolve to jump the many hurdles I encountered en route to completing it.

I ended up getting married before the book hit the shelves, gave birth to Sage, then devoted myself to raising her. I will never look back on Sage's childhood and think I didn't savor it while it was happening, and I am very proud of my accomplishments as a parent—but as Sage grew older, I had more free time on my hands and realized that my own life did not end at motherhood.

What would my next act be? I racked my brain and considered everything from other book ideas to starting an educational-video company geared toward toddlers. But nothing seemed to grab me the way that *New York Characters* did . . . until I thought of *Getting There*.

I realize now that I was so eager to produce this book and explore the paths people took to the top of their respective fields because, while I had certainly come a long way on my own winding path, I was still in need of mentors. Fortunately, I found them in spades.

My subjects demonstrated that success comes in a potpourri of flavors, that it can be achieved by a variety of different personality types, and that there are many roads to get there. They taught me that careers can have several chapters and that you don't need to know exactly where you want to end up when you start—in fact, most of the people in this book didn't. They took a first step, kept their eyes open for new opportunities, worked very hard (often for others, at least to start), and learned as they forged ahead.

- Leslie Moonves, the President and CEO of CBS, originally pursued acting
- Jim Koch credits his three-year stint as an outdoor-survival instructor for giving him the valuable tools and insights needed to create the Boston Beer Company
- Fitness guru Jillian Michaels only dedicated herself to that field after being fired as a talent agent
- craigslist founder Craig Newmark stumbled upon his businesses while trying to pursue a social goal

The most consistent refrain, stressed by almost everyone, is what Cathy mentioned and what my experience with *New York Characters* confirmed: You must do something that you are passionate about—and something that is "within your circle of competence," as Warren Buffett puts it. The road to get there is almost guaranteed to be arduous, but if you love what you do, you'll thrive on the inevitable challenges and have the stamina to achieve your potential.

- Author Jeff Kinney spent eight years writing his first *Diary of a Wimpy Kid* book
- John Paul DeJoria was fired from three jobs and lived in his car on two dollars and fifty cents a day before founding John Paul Mitchell Systems and, later, Patrón Spirits Company
- It took Jeff Koons nine years after graduating art school to make enough money from his art to give up having a second job
- After establishing his own architectural practice, Frank Gehry found himself on the verge of bankruptcy several times before reaching solid ground

Many of my subjects also emphasize the importance of not allowing rejection or the fear of failure to deter you. They believe that if you don't take risks you will never get any-where, and they view falling down as just part of the process. As super-model-turned-entrepreneurial-mogul Kathy Ireland succinctly puts it, "If you never fail, it means you are not trying hard enough." It's not surprising that several of my subjects credit jobs in sales (often door-to-door) for hammering these points home—so convincingly, in fact, that I would love for my daughter to have this experience someday.

Not only do my subjects share indispensable and practical career advice that is applicable to a wide range of fields—

- Michael Bloomberg gives tips on circumventing life's gatekeepers
- Anderson Cooper describes why sometimes you have to do something drastic to change the way others perceive you
- Spanx inventor Sara Blakely details why it's smart to keep a young entrepreneurial idea secret, even from friends and family
- *Mad Men* creator Matthew Weiner reveals how to process rejection
- Leading scientist J. Craig Venter demonstrates that just because most people do things a certain way, doesn't mean it's the best way

—but they also bestow loads of wisdom on a much grander scale.

- Warren Buffett explains the vast benefits of being a good communicator—and why the people you choose to surround yourself with, even as friends, affect your own behavior and destiny
- Leading trial lawyer David Boies discloses why it's often smart to listen as much as you can before speaking
- Hollywood film executive Stacey Snider explains how you can have it all by prioritizing different stages of your life
- Nitin Nohria, dean of Harvard Business School, spells out why one should go through life being generous and not keeping score

After completing this book and hearing so many people I admire describe their own trajectories in an honest, human, and identifiable way, I feel confident saying that no one sails through life without encountering some rough waters. No matter who you are, how far you've come on your own personal journey, or what you have achieved in your career, you can always benefit from a great role model. It's never too late to be inspired by these stories. It's never too late to improve. It's never too late to try something new. It's never too late to discover something about yourself.

# WARREN BUFFETT
## INVESTOR

**UP UNTIL THE AGE OF TWENTY, I WAS ABSOLUTELY UNABLE TO SPEAK IN PUBLIC.
JUST THE THOUGHT OF IT MADE ME PHYSICALLY ILL. I WOULD LITERALLY THROW UP.**
I selected courses in college where I didn't have to stand up in front of the class, and I arranged
my life so that I would never find myself in front of a crowd. If I somehow did, I could hardly
say my own name. I'm not sure what led to this problem, but it was there in a big way.

When I was at Columbia Business School, I saw an ad in the paper for a Dale Carnegie
public-speaking course and figured it would serve me well. I went to Midtown, signed up,
and gave them a check. But after I left, I swiftly stopped payment. I just couldn't do it. I was
that terrified. I returned to Omaha after graduating and got a job as a salesman of securities.
I knew that I had to be able to speak in front of people. So again, I saw an ad in the paper and
went down to sign up; but this time I handed the instructor one hundred dollars in cash. I
knew if I gave him the cash I'd show up. And I did.

There were about thirty other people in the class and we all had trouble saying our own
names. We met once a week for a dozen or so weeks. They would give us different types of
speeches to practice and taught us psychological tricks to overcome our fears. There was that
communal feeling that we were all in the same boat and really helped one another get through
the class. As soon as the course was over, I went to the University of Omaha and said, "I want
to start teaching." I knew that if I did not speak in front of people quickly I would lapse back
to where I'd started. I just kept doing it, and now you can't stop me from talking!

The impact that class had on my life was huge. In fact, I don't have my diploma from
the University of Nebraska hanging on my office wall, and I don't have my diploma from
Colombia up there either—but I do have my Dale Carnegie graduation certificate proudly

displayed. That $100 course gave me the most important degree I have. It's certainly had the biggest impact in terms of my subsequent success.

In graduate school you learn all this complicated stuff, but what's really essential is being able to get others to follow your ideas. If you're a salesperson, you want people to follow your advice. If you're a management leader, you want them to follow you in business. Whatever you do, good communication skills are incredibly important and something that almost anybody can improve upon, both in writing and speaking. A relatively modest improvement can make a major difference in your future earning power, as well as in many other aspects of your life. In my case, I proposed to my wife during the time I was taking the public-speaking course. Who knows, but maybe if I had been talking in my voice of six months earlier I wouldn't have persuaded her to say yes. There are all kinds of good things that come out of sound communication skills.

One of the best things you can do in life is to surround yourself with people who are better than you are. High-grade people. You will end up behaving more like them, and they, in turn, will get it back from you. It's like a planetary system. If you hang around with people who behave worse than you, pretty soon you'll start being pulled in that direction. That's just the way it seems to work. Who you choose to associate with matters.

It's also imperative to select the right heroes. I have always been lucky in that respect. The people you look up to will form your vision of how you want to be in later life. I've had a number of terrific heroes who have never let me down. I've been able to pick up all sorts of valuable things from them.

My first hero was my dad. I grew up with this incredible love and admiration for him. I wanted to be like him. He gave me more good advice than anybody, and he was enormously helpful and important to me in all kinds of ways. He taught me that what's on your inner scorecard is more important than your outer scorecard. A lot of people are concerned with what the world will think about this or that instead of what they themselves think about it. If you are comfortable with your inner scorecard, you are going to have a pretty gratifying life. The people who strive too much for the outer scorecard sometimes find that it's a little hollow when they get through. My father died forty-six years ago. I have a large portrait of him on my office wall, and I still wonder how he would feel about anything I do.

The most important thing that ever happened to me was marrying Susie, another hero of mine. She had a terrific impact on me. In terms of living a happy life, it was night and day. I was not well-adjusted prior to meeting her. The biggest obstacle I had was a personality that hadn't fully developed, and that's a pretty big obstacle! I did not have the right social habits and wasn't very sensitive to how other people thought. I don't mean that I was completely in the other direction. I got along fine with a lot of people, but my social abilities lagged behind my intellectual ones. There was a lot of catching up to do, and it didn't happen overnight. It was as if Susie had a little watering can. She poured water on me and, after a long enough time, flowers bloomed where weeds used to grow. She took care of both the outer and inner me. I needed that. If not for Susie, I think I would probably have gone through life like many people do. I would have made a lot of money—it isn't like I needed help in that respect—and maybe I would have even become well-known, but I don't think I would have been happy. I would have been a mess.

You have lived a successful life if, as you grow older, the people who you hope love you actually do. I have never known anyone who does not feel like a success when they have gotten close to my age and have a lot of people who love them. I know enormously wealthy individuals who have dinners held in their honor, hospital wings named after them, and all that sort of thing, but the truth is that no one thinks much of them. I have to believe that at some point they realize it, and everything gets quite empty after that.

Benjamin Graham, my old boss and mentor, was another hero. He was a genius. I took a job with him when I was getting started and never even asked what the salary was going to be (I found that out at the end of the month when I got my paycheck). Try to work for whomever you admire most. It won't necessarily be the job that you'll have ten years later, but you'll have the opportunity to pick up so much as you go along. You don't want to take a job just for the money, and you should never work for people who make your stomach churn or who keep you up at night. If you are in a situation like that, think about changing it. And make sure you follow your passion—whatever turns you on. You want to be excited when you get out of bed in the morning. I tap dance to work every day, and I work with people I think are terrific.

When Ben was about twelve years old, he determined that it would be best to go through life with people liking and admiring him. He came to this conclusion not only because of how it would make him feel but also because it would make getting people to accept his ideas easier. So he sat down and wrote a list of the positive qualities in the people he looked up to. He then wrote a list of the negative qualities in the people who turned him off. When Ben reviewed these two lists, he realized that none of the attractive characteristics were impossible for him to obtain, and none of the negative ones were impossible for him to reject. They were qualities of behavior and character, not things like the ability to kick a football sixty yards or jump seven feet in the air. So Ben consciously decided to become the type of person he admired.

Qualities of good character and integrity make an enormous difference in achieving success. I urge students to conduct various forms of Ben's exercise. Most behavior is habitual. They say the chains of habit are too light to be felt until they are too heavy to be broken. There's no question about it. I see older people entrapped by self-destructive behavior patterns all the time. Bad habits are hard to kick, but good habits are too. So why not decide to

have good habits? And form them as soon as you can. When you get to be my age, it's a lot tougher to do.

My good friend and hero, Tom Murphy, had an incredible generosity of spirit. He would do five things for you without thinking about whether you did something for him. After he was done with those five things, he'd be thinking about how to do the sixth. He was also an enormously able person in business and was kind of effortless about it. He didn't have to shout or scream or anything like that. He did everything in a very relaxed manner. Forty years ago, Tom gave me one of the best pieces of advice I've ever received. He said, "Warren, you can always tell someone to go to hell tomorrow." It's such an easy way of putting it. You haven't missed the opportunity. Just forget about it for a day. If you feel the same way tomorrow, tell them then—but don't spout off in a moment of anger.

My brain is not a general-purpose brain that works marvelously in all situations. There are all sorts of things that I'm no good at. My son can do things with music that I couldn't do in a million years. I can't play football well; I never could. I can't play chess like other people can. But my mind does work well in terms of evaluating businesses. I have this one little skill, and I was dropped into a society where it's paid off in a huge, huge way. That being said, there are still all kinds of investment opportunities I'm not able to comprehend. I understand some kinds of simple businesses. I can't understand complicated ones. Coca-Cola, for example, isn't very complicated. It's a durable product and the appeal is universal. I try to find businesses I can grasp, where I like the people running them and think the price makes sense in relation to the future economics. I believe very strongly in operating within what I call my "circle of competence." The most important thing in terms of your circle of competence is not how large it is but how well you define the perimeter. If you know where your edges are, you are way better off than somebody who has a circle five times as large but is very fuzzy about the border. Knowing what to leave out is as important as knowing what to focus on. Tom Watson, the founder of IBM, put it best. He said, "I'm no genius, but I'm smart in spots, and I stay around those spots."

An important quality in my field is emotional stability. You have to be able to think independently. If I take a poll on every investment decision I make, I'm going to be doing exactly what everyone else is, and I usually don't think much of that. As your company gets larger and you have larger groups making decisions, the decisions get more homogenized. I don't think you will ever get brilliant investment decisions out of a large committee. I must have a temperament that lets me think for myself. When I come to a conclusion, I can't be bothered if others disagree with me. That's tough for a lot of people, but as long as I feel that I know the facts, I'm okay with it.

In the investment or business world, you have to be able to pull the trigger when you have a good idea and you've got to be willing to do it big. I usually don't have any troubles in that department. My personality goes down that line. But I've still made a few major mistakes of omission. There have been things that I've known enough about but either didn't participate in or did on a small scale. I was sucking my thumb, basically, instead of writing checks. There is no place that lists "missed opportunities," but I have passed up some big ones.

I have also made some bad investments. There is no question that you are going to make mistakes in life. I've made a lot, and I'm going to make more. You just have to make sure that your blunders are never fatal, and you don't want to make them on the really big decisions. For example, choosing the person you marry. I may try to minimize my errors, but I'm not one to dwell on them. It isn't worth it. You have to put your mistakes behind you and not look back. Tomorrow is another day. Just go on to the next thing and strive to do your best.

It's important to realize that others are going to make mistakes too. There is no way that anyone's going to make a lot of business decisions without messing up on occasion so I have to decide if the people working for me know what they are doing overall. I'm not big on blame and, by other people's standards, I'm probably quite tolerant of our managers' mistakes.

The triumphs in life are triumphs because you know that not everything is going to be one. If you played golf and got a hole in one on every hole, you'd get bored. Part of the fun is hitting one into the woods and then getting a great recovery shot. And sometimes you don't get great recovery shots. To me, making money is an interesting game. The reason I continue is similar to why top golfers keep playing. They're not doing it for the money; it's for the love of the sport. There are a lot of people out there doing what I do, so it's exciting for me to be competing and doing well.

## WARREN'S PEARLS

■ Toward the end of college, I fixed my ambitions on attending Harvard Business School. I was almost certain that they would accept me. On the day of my big interview, I woke before dawn and caught a ten-hour train to Chicago. I then switched to a little inner-urban train—so it was another hour up to meet the alumnus who was interviewing me. We spoke for about ten minutes, he assessed my capabilities, and he turned me down on the spot. They didn't even send me a letter later on; it was crushing. My dad had always had these high expectations for me, so on my ride home I had about eleven hours to think about the fact that he was going to be disappointed. I felt terrible; it was that feeling of dread. But almost immediately I started investigating other schools and discovered that Benjamin Graham, whose book I had recently read and loved, was teaching at Columbia. I ended up being accepted by Columbia, Graham became a major influence in my life, and the rest is history.

It's been my general experience that things that seem disastrous at the time usually do work out for the best. My rejection from Harvard is certainly a dramatic illustration of this.

- Reputation is very important. I ask the managers of my companies to judge every action that they take not just by legal standards (which, of course, is the first test) but also by what I call the "newspaper test." How would they feel about every given action if they knew it would show up the next day in their local paper, written by a smart but kind of unfriendly reporter and read by their families, friends, and neighbors? If it passes that test, it's okay. If anything is close to the line, it's out.

- Most people go through life using up a very, very small part of their potential. You could have a three-hundred-horsepower motor and get three hundred horsepower out of it or you can get a lot less. The people who I see function well are not the ones with the biggest "motors," but the ones with the most efficient ones.

- Here's a message that I think is very important to get across to younger people. I express it to them like this: "Every fifteen-year-old boy and most fifteen-year-old girls are constantly thinking, *When do I get my first car and what will it be?* Let's say that I offer to buy you the car of your dreams. You can pick out any car that you want, and when you get out of class this afternoon, that car will be waiting for you at home. There's just one catch . . . It's the only car you're ever going to get in your entire life. Now, knowing that, how are you going to treat that car? You're probably going to read the owner's manual four times before you drive it; you're going to keep it in the garage, protect it at all times, change the oil twice as often as necessary. If there's the least little bit of rust, you're going to get that fixed immediately so it doesn't spread—because you know it has to last you as long as you live. Here's the thing, that's *exactly* the position you are in concerning your mind and body. You have only one mind and one body for the rest of your life. If you aren't taking care of them when you're sixteen or seventeen, it's like leaving that car out in hailstorms and letting rust eat away at it. If you don't take care of your mind and body now, by the time you are forty or fifty you'll be like a car that can't go anywhere. So isn't it just as important to take care of your mind and body as it is to take care of that car?" They seem to get that.

# MATTHEW WEINER
## MAD MEN CREATOR

**I REMEMBER STUDYING SAMUEL TAYLOR COLERIDGE'S POEM "KUBLA KHAN" IN HIGH SCHOOL. ACCORDING TO COLERIDGE, UPON WAKING FROM A DEEP, OPIUM-INDUCED** reverie, he recalled a vision and immediately wrote the fifty-four famous lines. But when we started doing the poetic analysis, it became clear that there was no way this poem came out all at once. It has this amazing structure. We learned from letters and notes that had been discovered that it was likely Coleridge had not only worked on "Kubla Khan" for several months but that he also sent it to friends for feedback.

Artists frequently hide the steps that lead to their masterpieces. They want their work and their career to be shrouded in the mystery that it all came out at once. It's called hiding the brushstrokes, and those who do it are doing a disservice to people who admire their work and seek to emulate them. If you don't get to see the notes, the rewrites, and the steps, it's easy to look at a finished product and be under the illusion that it just came pouring out of someone's head like that. People who are young, or still struggling, can get easily discouraged because they can't do it like they thought it was done. An artwork is a finished product, and it should be, but I always swore to myself that I would not hide my brushstrokes.

Writers were revered in my home and I wanted to be one since I was a kid, but when I went to college, I could not get into a writing class. I went to Wesleyan, a very small liberal arts school. The classes had only twelve to fifteen people, and you had to submit writing samples to get in. Mine, apparently, were just not good enough. I was rejected from every writing class. I ended up convincing an English teacher to do a one-on-one independent poetry study with me. When I finished my thesis, I was extremely proud and wanted others

to see it. I gave it to a humanities professor and he invited me to his house to read the work out loud. After the first poem, he told me to get out a pen and take notes. He began, "The infantile use of . . . The puerile . . . The childish use of . . . The cliché awkwardness . . . " It was one humiliating cruelty after the next. And I had to write these insults down myself. I literally went through hours of this, poem after poem. He finally leaned over to me and said, "I think you know that you are not a poet." I said, "I was not aware of that."

While being battered always hurts, an important survival mechanism I've acquired over the years is to both thrive on rejection and hold on to compliments. Rejection enrages me, but that "I'll show you!" feeling is an extremely powerful motivator. I'm at a point now where I'm afraid that if I lose it I'll stop working. On the flip side, there's nothing like a meaningful compliment from someone you respect. In my youth I was a miserable student and rarely did my homework. My fourth grade teacher once pulled me aside and let me have it. She said, "Talking to you is like talking down the drain; you don't hear anything. You think you are going to make it through the rest of your life because you are charming. You think you don't have to do all the work—but you do." I remember looking up at her after this tirade and saying, "You think I'm charming?"

After college, I attended film school at the University of Southern California, where I finally started doing some narrative writing. There were contests for the films that the school would actually make, and my material was never selected. I finally said, "I am going to make a documentary," and made one about the paparazzi. It stood out and I became known for my editing skills and sense of humor. Upon graduation, I set up meetings everywhere in the hopes of getting a job. In three months I got nothing. I couldn't even get a meeting with an agent.

So for the next three years I stayed home and wrote spec scripts. My friends had day jobs, but I didn't. My wife, Linda, worked hard as an architect and supported us. I attempted to shop my material around, but nothing sold. I got very bitter, seeing people I didn't think deserved it succeed. It was a dark time. Show business looked so impenetrable that I eventually stopped writing. I began watching TV all day and lying about it. My mother would call me to drive my brother-in-law to the airport. That's the kind of crap I was doing instead of being a writer. I felt like the most useless, worthless person in the world.

Then one day I saw the low-budget movie *Clerks*. It inspired me to get off my ass and make my own independent film: a small, quirky comedy where I played myself—a failing screenwriter. I used my wife, my apartment, my car—basically everything I could to finish the film. Making that movie was a transformational experience. It had trouble getting into festivals and never sold, but I had set out to do something and had gotten it done.

A friend of mine from college had a pilot in the works that needed punch-up. Punch-up is a bunch of comedy writers sitting around the room making a script funnier. I didn't even know there was such a job, but I got to drive onto the Warner Bros. lot and sit in this room with all these professional writers. It turned out that I was pretty good at it. Everything I said was included in the script, and that felt great. The showrunner came up to me afterward and offered me $600 if I could stay through the end of the pilot. I was like, "Oh, my God. Yes. I'll be here." I would've done it for free just to be able to drive onto the lot again. That show quickly went off the air but word had gotten out that I was funny. Another showrunner took me to lunch and hired me for his show. One job leads to another, but you have to start somewhere. It was my first paying job in show business and I was thirty.

Comedy hours are long—literally fourteen-hour days, sometimes seven days a week. But I always wanted to create my own show, so I started researching my "advertising project" (*Mad Men*) in my spare time. It was like having a mistress. I worked on it at night or during my off-hours when I was not with my family. I paid people to do research, inundated myself with material, and even hired a writer's assistant to dictate to because I was too tired to type (it also freed my imagination). When I finished the script, I felt like it was something special.

I sent it off to my agent and pitched it to everyone I could. I literally carried it in my bag wherever I went in case I ran into someone who might be useful. I wasn't able to get meetings at the big networks, but I pitched it to small production companies. From them, I heard things like "You don't know what you're doing." "Are you aware of how uncommercial this is?" "Are you pulling our leg?" But, honestly, the most stinging responses I heard were along the lines of "This is one of the most beautiful, well-executed, exciting things I've ever read, but I'm afraid that we just don't do this kind of show." Those comments made me feel as if I were alone in the universe.

One person my agent sent *Mad Men* to was David Chase, the creator of *The Sopranos*. All I wanted was for him to read it and maybe godfather it into HBO, but he liked it so much he decided to hire me. He said, "Even if I fire you, I'm going to help you make this." And he actually gave it to HBO, but they passed because they didn't want to do a period piece.

Obviously, I continued to pitch *Mad Men* everywhere. Showtime, Lionsgate, Sony, FX—all of them passed. *Mad Men* had been bouncing around town for about four years and nobody wants something that has been rejected by everybody.

But then along came AMC. They were trying to make a splash and wanted to do something new. They were also interested in making a show they wanted to watch, which is really the secret of success in everything artistic. They basically said, "We love this thing and want to do it." I was so excited—but at that time no one thought AMC was, in show biz terms, a "somebody." Everybody felt sorry for me. I can't even tell you the pity I got. It was as if I were taking my project and screening it in someone's basement. No one even knew that channel. But AMC gave me complete creative control and all I remember thinking was *I'm going to live my dream*.

It took seven years from the time I wrote *Mad Men* until it finally got on the screen. I lived every day with that script as if it were going to happen tomorrow. That's the faith you have to have.

Hollywood is tough, but I do believe that if you are truly talented, get your material out there, can put up with the rejection, and don't set a time limit for yourself, someone will notice you.

The most defeatist thing I hear is "I'm going to give it a couple of years." You can't set a clock for yourself. If you do, you are not a writer. You should want it so badly that you don't have a choice. You have to commit for the long haul. There's no shame in being a starving artist. Get a day job, but don't get too good at it. It will take you away from your writing.

The greatest regret I have is that, early in my career, I showed myself such cruelty for not having accomplished anything significant. I spent so much time trying to write, but was paralyzed by how behind I felt. Many years later I realized that if I had written only a couple of pages a day I would've written five hundred pages at the end of a year (and that's not even working weekends). Any contribution you make on a daily basis is fantastic. I still happen to write almost everything at once, but I now cut myself slack on all of the thinking and procrastination time I use. I know that it's all part of my creative process.

## MATTHEW'S PEARLS

■ When you have a meeting with somebody, look that person up and know everything you can about him or her. It's pretty effortless and can pay dividends. This might seem basic, but for some reason it took me forever to get it.

■ Remember people's names and don't be insulted if they don't return the favor. If you know someone's name, you can own them. I read that Napoleon used this trick. He spent huge amounts of time committing his soldiers' names to memory—and they would die for him.

■ When you are starting out, you have to enter contests and send your material to people cold. Send it to people who are in the business of looking at new ideas. You must also be in the industry's city to network and schmooze. You have to make connections to people, and no matter how early they are in their career, treat them as if they were important. They might be one day.

■ When someone rejects your work, register the fact that they don't like it, but don't listen to the reason why. People feel that they have to say something, and they often give a capricious justification to keep from hurting your feelings. For example, someone might say, "I don't like your movie because it's in black-and-white." You think, *Damn it. If I had made it in color, I could've sold it.* That's probably not true. Now, if William Goldman or Mike Nichols reads your work and suggests you do X to it, you might want to listen, but if you alter your work for every rejection, you'll end up running in all different directions trying to please an imaginary audience. It can be damaging and destructive.

■   A great idea is worthless; execution is everything. It does not matter if you invented *Star Wars* before *Star Wars* existed. You might get some money from selling your idea, but it will never amount to much. Actually write the script. There's no arguing with an existing piece of material, and you don't have to rely on anyone else's imagination.

# MICHAEL BLOOMBERG

## BLOOMBERG L.P. FOUNDER / FORMER NEW YORK CITY MAYOR

**IN COLLEGE I HAD A STRAIGHT C AVERAGE. I THINK I WAS I JUST LAZY, OR MAYBE I WAS JUST TOO BUSY CHASING THE GIRLS. BUT THEN, FIRST SEMESTER SENIOR YEAR,** I figured that if I wanted to go to graduate school I'd better do something about my grades. So for that one semester I took a double course load and got all A's. I applied to business school and I got in, much to everybody's amazement, particularly mine. Then I went right back to getting C's for my last semester.

After graduation, I thought I was going to serve in Vietnam. In those days everybody was going to Vietnam. But they wouldn't take me at the last minute because I have flat feet. Why it bothered them, I don't know. So I needed to find a job all of a sudden. I went to work on Wall Street only because a friend of mine said, "Call these two firms—Goldman Sachs & Co. and Salomon Brothers & Hutzler (as it was called back then)—and tell them you want to be a trader or a salesman."

Fortunately for me, securities trading and sales were considered second-class occupations in those days, so I got interviews at both firms. At Goldman I was introduced to the managing partner like this: "Mr. Levy, this is Mike Bloomberg." At Salomon Brothers I was introduced to some guy named Billy. We had a discussion, and afterward somebody came up to me and said, "What'd Billy Salomon have to say?" I had just been introduced to the managing partner on a first-name basis! I felt that Salomon Brothers was the place for me. To say I fit in there and loved what I was doing is an understatement. I reveled in it every minute of the day. But the thing is, fifteen years later, they fired me.

I was fired around the time the company was sold. They assembled an executive committee of seven people that decided who stayed and who went. One of the committee members did not like me—my crime being that I had been the assistant to his nemesis—and he convinced everyone else to vote against me. He was later killed in a plane crash, and the other six members of the executive committee became paying customers of mine.

As somebody once said, "Living well is the best revenge."

I don't remember being too pissed or feeling that bad about being fired. I think I have the same insecurities that everybody else has. The difference is that I don't let them get in my way. There's a great scene in the movie *The Sting* between Paul Newman's and Robert Redford's characters. They rob a bank and in the midst of doing this somebody points a gun at Newman. Afterward, Redford asks him if he was scared. Newman replies, "Right down to my boots."

As long as you can admit things to yourself, you can deal with them and then move on. I don't lie to myself, but I don't harp on things and I never, ever look back. If your mind starts to wander to past events, the only advice I can give you is *don't go. Just stop it!* Think about something else. If you divert your attention, your mind won't immediately go back to the unpleasant occurrence, and when it eventually does, simply stop thinking about it again. That's how you quit smoking. You don't have to stop for the rest of your life, just stop for five minutes. Five minutes from now you probably won't want a cigarette. If you do, force yourself to stop for another five. Eventually, one of these fives will end in not wanting a cigarette. And then one day you'll think, *I've come so far and I don't want go back.*

Had a place like Goldman Sachs called me after I was fired from Salomon and wanted to make me a partner, I would've done it. But nobody offered me a job. Thank God for that! I started my own company instead.

I like that old Woody Allen quote: "Eighty percent of success is just showing up." You create your own lot in life, and to be successful in business you've got to work hard. The more you work, the better you do. It's that simple. Some people say, "I can't go into work today." I've never missed a day of work in my life! After I was fired from Salomon, I still had about two months left before I was actually going to leave the firm, but I still never missed a day. In fact, I made sure that I worked six days a week from as early in the morning until as late as I could. I was searching for new office space for myself during that period, but I called the broker and said I could only look on weekends because I didn't want to take time off during the week. I didn't want anyone to ever say that I didn't work 110 percent. I had an ego problem with that.

Be the first one in and the last one out. If you are there early and stay late, you get a chance to talk to people who would not otherwise take your call. I built many relationships by being early. You can call the chairman of the board of almost any company early in the morning. If he's a good chairman, he's there. The secretary's not, so he'll actually answer the phone. The best time to strike is when gatekeepers aren't there! When I started developing Bloomberg, I wanted feedback. So every morning I'd arrive at the deli across the street from Merrill Lynch's headquarters at six a.m. and buy coffee (with and without milk) and tea (with and without milk), plus a few sugars on the side. I'd go up and roam the halls looking to see if there happened to be somebody sitting in their office alone reading a newspaper. I'd walk in and say, "Hi, I'm Mike Bloomberg. I bought you a cup of coffee. I'd just like to bend your ear." Nobody is going to say, "Get outta here" if you just bought him or her a cup of coffee. When someone would occasionally say, "I don't drink coffee," I would say, "Well, then have a tea."

Over the years, people have come to me and said, "You can't do everything." That is total bullshit. You certainly can do everything. The people who do some things can do more. If you need to get something tough done, give it to the most overworked person in your organization. There's a reason why they're overworked; they get things done. I have an employee named Patti Harris; she should be written about instead of me. She runs my foundation, she runs the city, she has a husband, they have a great marriage, she's got a great family (the kids turned out spectacularly), they go on vacations, they ski, they scuba dive. If you go up to her with doubts that something can be accomplished because of this obstacle or that obstacle, she'll look at you, smile, and say, "That's nice, just do it," and walk away.

My parents were my role models. My father was a bookkeeper for a little dairy company. He worked seven days a week until he checked himself into the hospital to die. At that point my mother knew that she would have to start driving. She went to the library, checked out a book on driving, took the car onto our little street, and taught herself how to drive. She got a friend to take her to the DMV, took the test, and got her license. That was it. *She just did it.*

After running Bloomberg for twenty years, I decided it was time to do something different. Time to fire myself. I wanted to turn over the company to others without anyone thinking I was walking away from it. Well, public service is a good excuse, and it's of great interest to me. People say that government can't be made to work efficiently and truly serve the people. My response? "Bullshit!" Telling me something's impossible is like waving a red flag in front of a bull. Might as well go for it. So that's what I'm working toward now.

## MICHAEL'S PEARLS

■ People want recognition and respect. When I walk into a building, I always make a point of shaking the hands of the security people at the door. If it wasn't for them, the rest of us wouldn't be able to conduct our business. They are just as important as the head of the company. I think the egalitarian concept that America was built around really works. We have grown to have too many distinctions between people. It's important to recognize when credit is due and not be stingy about giving it.

■ Use the words "we" and "us" when referring to your business. Never use "I" and "me." It sounds egotistical.

# SARA BLAKELY
## SPANX INVENTOR

**FOR AS LONG AS I CAN REMEMBER, I WANTED TO BE A TRIAL ATTORNEY. ALL MY DECISIONS WERE MADE WITH THAT GOAL IN MIND. IT WAS MY FATHER'S PROFESSION AND,** as a child, I used to beg to watch him in court. During closing arguments, he'd take me out of school and I'd sit there all day, taking notes on different jury members. I loved every minute of it.

I debated in high school and continued in college where I also majored in legal communications. Eventually, the time came for me to take the LSAT, and I did *horribly*. I'm a terrible test taker. My reading comprehension is not great, and I have trouble focusing for long periods of time. Doing so poorly on the test was beyond devastating, but I scraped myself up off the floor, enrolled in an LSAT prep course, studied my ass off, and took the test again.

I did one point worse.

Traumatized, I wondered, *What is the universe trying to tell me?*—'cause that's kind of how I look at things. In my mind the universe was now telling me to drive to Disney World and audition for the role of Goofy. That is literally how I responded to my defeat. But they only audition people for the character roles every once in a while, so in the meantime I got a job at Epcot.

When I finally tried out to be Goofy, they said I was too short to wear the costume and made me a chipmunk instead. I didn't actually end up playing the chipmunk. The way Disney worked was that you had to stay where you were initially employed for a period of time before you were allowed to transfer positions. So I continued to wear my brown polyester "space suit" and put people on Epcot rides. I had to walk on a moving sidewalk for eight

hours a day and say, "Hi, welcome to Disney, watch your step please." I'd see school friends, and they'd look at my big Mickey Mouse name tag, and be, like, "Sara? Sara Blakely? Is that you?" I'd sheepishly say, "Yeah, just get on the ride." After three months of this, I'd had my fill of "the happiest place on earth" and decided to return home and live with my mom.

Still without much direction, I got a job at a local company selling fax machines door-to-door. It was the kind of place that would hire anyone with a pulse. On my first day they handed me a phone book and said, "Here are your four zip codes, get out there and sell." There was no list of accounts that were likely to buy from me. I had to 100 percent drum up my own leads. I would wake up in the morning and drive around cold-calling from eight until five. Most doors were slammed in my face. I saw my business card ripped up at least once a week, and I even had a few police escorts out of buildings. It wasn't long before I grew immune to the word "no" and even found my situation amusing. I realized that I can find humor in almost anything and, needing some sort of creative outlet, I began to dabble in stand-up comedy at night.

I think recreationally, if that makes any sense. I'll sit on the couch and three hours will go by when I'm lost in thought. What I've realized is that I'm a visualizer. It's not meditation, and I don't do it for any set period of time—it's just sort of been a part of my existence, like a long-standing hobby. During my fax-selling stint, I would spend much of my free time trying to figure out what I really wanted out of life and what my strengths were. I knew I was good at selling and that I eventually wanted to be self-employed. I thought, *Instead of fax machines, I'd love to sell something that I created and actually care about.* I became very specific with my visualizations and even wrote in my journal that I wanted to start a business that could run on its own whether I was physically present or not.

One day, after about seven years of selling fax machines, something fortuitous happened. In the hopes of looking better in my fitted white pants, I cut the feet out of a pair of pantyhose and substituted them for my underwear. This allowed me to benefit from the slimming effects of the panty hose's "control top" while allowing my feet to go bare in my cute sandals. The moment I saw how good my butt looked, I was like, "Thank you, God, *this* is my opportunity!" I would create a unique type of body shapewear, something that would be thin, comfortable, and invisible under clothes but would still perform the magic of a girdle. It was the business I had been mentally laying the groundwork for all this time.

For the first full year I kept my idea a secret from anyone who could not directly help to move it forward. That was my gut instinct at the time, but it's now one of the best pieces of advice I have to give. Ideas are the most vulnerable at the moment you have them; that's also the time people are most inclined to run around seeking validation from everyone they know. Discouraging remarks will likely take you off course. You'll either end up deflated or spend your time defending your idea instead of going for it. I worked on Spanx until I felt I had enough of myself invested that I wouldn't turn back regardless of what I heard. Everyone in my life knew I was pursuing an "idea" (I had to tell them something because I went to the Georgia Tech library almost every night and weekend to work on it), but they had no clue what it was. When I finally sat my friends and family down and said, "Okay, it's footless pantyhose!" they thought I was joking and laughed hysterically. Out of love, I heard things like "Well, honey, if it's a good idea why haven't the big guys done it?" and "Even if it does turn out to be a good idea, the big guys will knock you off right away." I told them, "You may be right, but I've just spent a year researching this, patenting it, naming it, and creating the package. I'm already on my path and I'm not getting off now." I'm pretty positive that if I had told my friends and family about Spanx early on I'd still be selling fax machines.

The problem was that even those who could help Spanx advance were discouraging. I couldn't move forward without a prototype, and I needed a factory to produce one. I began by calling the local mills but, without exception, they either laughed at me or explained that it was a dumb idea that would never sell. So I decided to draw on a lesson I learned during my cold-calling days: Face-to-face makes a huge difference. I took a week off work and drove around North Carolina popping by many of the same mills that had already rejected me via phone. I would literally sit in their lobby and wait to speak to either the founder or owner. I usually got about five minutes to make my pitch but, once again, no one was interested.

About two to three weeks after this unfruitful trip, a mill owner in Charlotte called and said, "Sara, I've decided to help make your crazy idea." When I asked him why he had the change of heart, he replied, "I have three daughters." I think he was both won over by my passion and had developed a soft spot in his heart from imagining his daughters in my shoes one day.

My own father also played an important role in my success. When my brother and I were growing up, he would encourage us to fail. We'd sit around the dinner table and he'd ask, "What did you guys fail at this week?" If we had nothing to tell him, he'd be disappointed. The logic seems counterintuitive, but it worked beautifully. He knew that many people become paralyzed by the fear of failure. They're constantly afraid of what others will think if they don't do a great job and, as a result, take no risks. My father wanted us to try everything and feel free to push the envelope. His attitude taught me to define failure as not trying something I want to do instead of not achieving the right outcome.

I believe that defeat is life's way of nudging you and letting you know you're off course. There's always some sort of hidden opportunity or lesson in each episode—a chance to build your character. Spanx wouldn't exist if I had aced the LSAT.

From cold-calling I learned that you have about fifteen seconds to capture someone's attention—but if you can make them smile or laugh, you get an extra fifteen to thirty. When I invented Spanx, I didn't have the money to grab people's attention the conventional way:

through advertising. I needed to somehow inspire people to want to talk about pantyhose, one of the world's most boring topics. By infusing humor wherever I could (from naming it Spanx to writing "We've got your butt covered!" on the package), I ended up turning my product into something people love to joke about, and it has been referenced everywhere from *The Oprah Winfrey Show* to *Sex and the City*.

I can't tell you how many women come up to me and say something like "I've been cutting the feet out of my pantyhose for years. Why didn't I end up being the Spanx girl?" The reason is that a good idea is just a starting point. Everybody has them all day long; everybody has a multimillion-dollar idea inside. Edison said, "Genius is one percent inspiration and ninety-nine percent perspiration." The same holds true for innovation, invention, and entrepreneurialism. The combination of not being fazed by the word "no," tinkering with comedy, visualizing the product, and not being afraid of failure was critical for the success of Spanx. I was prepared to perspire for this opportunity.

## SARA'S PEARL

■ I've been through a lot of trauma in my life. Most of it stemming from the unexpected tragic deaths of people I love and the very painful divorce of my parents when I was sixteen. Just before my dad left home, he handed me Dr. Wayne Dyer's ten-tape series, *How to Be a No-Limit Person* and said, "I wish someone had given this to me when I was your age."

I now tell people that one of the most important things they can do for themselves and their children is to listen to that series. Society constantly assaults us with negative imagery and messages. You have to go out of your way to view things in a positive light. People go to chiropractors to align their backs, but it's also important to align your thinking from time to time. Listening to *How to Be a No-Limit Person* is my method. It has been emotionally encouraging, gotten me through the toughest of times, and framed my thinking in a way that helped lead to the success of Spanx. I still listen to it a couple of times a year.

# ANDERSON COOPER
# JOURNALIST

**MY FATHER DIED DURING HEART BYPASS SURGERY WHEN I WAS TEN YEARS OLD. WHEN I WAS TWENTY-ONE, MY TWENTY-THREE-YEAR-OLD BROTHER COMMITTED SUICIDE.**
He jumped off the terrace of our family's penthouse apartment as my mother pleaded for him to stay put. I think that anytime you experience traumatic loss early on it changes who you are and drastically affects your view of the world. At least that was the case with me.

My brother's death occurred the summer before my senior year of college, and I spent the remainder of my time at school reeling from it. I retreated emotionally as I attempted to understand what had happened and why. I was worried about my mom and even had serious doubts about my ability to survive and operate in the world. So when graduation rolled around, I felt lost, to say the least. I asked my mother what she thought I should do for work. "Follow your bliss," she said, quoting Joseph Campbell. But what was "my bliss"?

I remember making a list of all the attributes I wanted in a career and all the things I wanted out of life: *I didn't want to wake up at sixty and be in a gray suit in a gray office or a gray cubicle. I wanted to do something that had a purpose. I wanted to lead an interesting life. I wanted to learn new things every day. I wanted to travel.* But even though I was in touch with what I wanted, I had trouble taking a first step. I felt that any move I made would close off other opportunities, and I became obsessed with the notion of keeping my options open. This turned into a kind of paralysis that took me almost a year to get over.

I knew rationally that my fear of taking a step didn't make sense. I had talked to enough successful people to know that the path to success is often meandering. It can appear to be a

series of random events and only in retrospect can one look back and connect the dots. That knowledge was very comforting and eventually helped free me from the idea that whatever choice you make at age twenty-one or twenty-two really matters. It doesn't really matter. When I was in school I used to think that there was some sort of permanent record, like I would be continually judged for all my actions. But there is no permanent record. I've never been in a job interview where anyone has asked me for my grades in college or how I did on the SAT.

When I was growing up, news, and to some extent war, had always been a part of my life. I have fond memories of watching the CBS evening news with my family every night at dinner. As a child, I collected toy soldiers and weapons. In high school and college I took it upon myself to read a lot about the Vietnam War and I was especially interested in the foreign correspondents and photographers who covered it. Working as a foreign correspondent seemed like a very worthwhile adventure and something I realized I wanted to do. News, however, proved to be a hard business to break into.

I applied for an entry-level job at ABC doing basic office tasks—photocopying and answering phones—but I couldn't even get an interview. I think they were mildly interested but they were going through a hiring freeze at the time. I applied to a couple of other networks, but to no avail. I thought, *Such is the value of a Yale education!* It was depressing and it seemed like the end of the road.

A kid I had gone to high school with was working at Channel One, an agency that produces a youth-oriented news program broadcast to many high schools across America, and he was nice enough to alert me to an opening for a fact-checker. I was desperate to get my foot in any door, so I applied for the job and got it. I fact-checked for six months, but I saw no path to becoming a foreign correspondent anywhere in sight.

I'm a big believer in creating your own opportunity if no one gives you one. When you work at a company, people there tend to see you a certain way. In my case, they viewed me as a fact-checker—so the notion that I could be a reporter didn't occur to anybody. Had I asked, they would have probably said no because I wasn't on the right career path. Sometimes you have to do something drastic to change people's perception of you. For me, that was hatching a plan to quit my job as a fact-checker and go overseas to shoot stories by myself. I would make the stories as interesting and dangerous as possible, and then offer them to Channel One for such a low price that the stories would be hard to refuse. I knew I could live so cheaply overseas that it wouldn't matter how little I earned. A friend agreed to make me a fake press pass and loan me his home video camera. I didn't really know what I was doing, but I figured I'd learn along the way.

For my first story, I flew to Thailand and met up with some Burmese refugees who were working to overthrow their country's military dictatorship. They agreed to sneak me into Burma and hook me up with some students who were under fire. The story was compelling;

my roll of the dice paid off; and Channel One bought my video. After I freelanced this way for about a year, Channel One finally hired me as a full-time correspondent. I worked there for about two and a half years, filming stories from a variety of war-torn regions around the globe, including Somalia, Bosnia, and Rwanda. I continued to shoot on a home video camera and travel alone, but at least someone else was picking up the bills.

I used to experience tremendous anxiety before each trip. There was something about untethering from my familiar surroundings that got to me. Traveling by myself for indefinite periods of time, I went to remote locations where I could have very easily disappeared. It felt as if I were floating in space without any support.

When I landed in a developing country, the challenge continued. Living on about five dollars a day, I slept in dingy hotels with cockroaches crawling on the walls and camped out on roofs of buildings. I would go weeks at a time without talking to people and I clung to a makeshift routine for stability: Lunch at noon. Dinner at six. I remember once seeing Christiane Amanpour in Somalia. She had a vehicle and was accompanied by a whole crew. That kind of career seemed so far away from anything I was doing. I was just this kid with a home video camera. It was very trying and lonely.

When I would return home, I still felt alone. My friends were moseying along, living their lives, and, understandably, couldn't relate to the world I had been living in. Coming from some transformational two weeks where I'd seen malnourished children die before my eyes, stepped over decaying bodies in the street, been shot at by snipers, and met remarkable people facing huge obstacles, I couldn't really relate to my friends' world either. It was as if we no longer spoke the same language.

I was miserable a lot of the time, but even so, I knew that this was the career for me. The more I saw, the more I needed to see. There was no place I wouldn't go. I didn't let risks get in the way and I couldn't imagine doing anything else. I know this sounds irrational, but I literally felt as if I had no other options. It wasn't as if I were dabbling in this. I felt as if I didn't have a choice. It had to work out. There was no Plan B.

I would never have been as driven to do this kind of work had I not experienced such intense personal loss. When my father died, the world suddenly seemed like a scary place. I didn't feel that I could rely on other people, and I became fearful of what else might happen. These emotions were compounded when my brother committed suicide. I wanted to become autonomous, prepare myself for any eventuality, and protect myself from further pain. I think that's part of what drew me to war zones and other places where people's whole lives have been turned upside down. I wanted to learn about survival from those who were still standing. I also felt comfortable, in a weird way, being in places where the language of loss was spoken. In America people aren't nearly as comfortable discussing it. I understood what the people were going through a lot better than I would have without experiencing what I did.

When my contract with Channel One expired, ABC finally hired me—as a correspondent. As it turned out, not getting that entry-level job there was the best thing that ever happened to me. Had I gotten it, I would have spent about two years as a desk assistant and then maybe worked my way up to, I don't know, production assistant? Movement at the networks at the time was glacial. You could be there for years before even being sent out to shoot a local story. There's no way I would have ever been made a full-time news correspondent after three years. There was no established, internal path to doing that.

I eventually moved on and got hired by CNN to anchor their morning show. Unfortunately, that didn't work out. I was really nervous and uncomfortable. My performance was just terrible and they very quickly started to think, *Why have we hired this guy?*

The thing with being fired is that no one tells you they're about to do it—you just get fired one day. In the news business they sometimes don't even fire you in person, you read about it in the paper instead. I didn't know how badly I was doing at CNN until about three months into it when I got sent to Afghanistan without a camera crew. I arrived in Afghanistan with just my little home video camera, called back to the office to retrieve my voice mail, and some other anchor answered my phone—in my office. He had taken over my office! It was only by volunteering for jobs that nobody else wanted that I was able to fight my way back. I started filling in on any anchoring slot I could get my hands on. I would fly into Atlanta and anchor eight-hour days on Saturday and Sunday, when no one else wanted to work. I was so motivated because I still viewed it as "I don't have another option. There is no Plan B."

I've tried to eliminate fear from my life as much as possible. If there's something I'm nervous about, I try to plunge head first into it. For instance, up until pretty recently, I've had a fear of speaking in front of a crowd. It would make me nervous, sweaty, and sick. I know this might seem strange because I've been on the air for years, but it's completely different with a camera and a small crew. It's very intimate and it always felt very natural—as if I were talking to only one person through the camera. Even a news set never made me nervous—it's just a dark room with a camera. But being in a room in front of thousands of people is a whole other thing. So over the last couple of years I started doing public-speaking events on weekends and in my spare time. I flew around the country and forced myself to do it, and it worked—I'm now able to speak in front of crowds.

I rarely ask people for advice or permission when I'm planning on doing something I feel strongly about. That only opens the plan up to be crapped on. Had I asked the producers at Channel One if they would be supportive of my going out to make war videos, they would probably have said no. It's easier to say no than it is to say yes, and they might not have wanted to feel responsible for me in any way. So I just did it. I think that's how I approach just about everything.

By the way, I did mention my plan to one or two Channel One colleagues and they all said things like "You'll never be on air" or "You'll never be hired as a correspondent here." Even once I got hired people said things like "Okay, so you are working for this little show that's seen in high schools, but you'll never get a job at a network" or "You're going to have to start doing something at a small local station in the United States if you're ever going to get a job at a major network." All of which was incorrect. I'd much rather follow my gut, do something, and if it doesn't work out, have it crapped on then.

It seems like a lot of people, especially young ones, are imbued with the sense that they can become successful (however they define it) in some sudden, magical way. Some people do. They make a reality show or a sex tape and become rich overnight. But that doesn't happen to the vast majority of people, nor is it ultimately the way you want to become successful. Most people sweat it out for years and encounter some degree of humiliation and failure along the way.

## ANDERSON'S PEARL

■  I tell journalism students that there are three main steps to take: First, figure out what gets your adrenaline going. Next, figure out a way to make a career out of your passion. And finally, outwork everyone around you. (Come in earlier, leave later, and volunteer for everything that others don't want to do. Don't wait to be asked to do something. Take it upon yourself and do it.) But you're only going to be able to outwork others if you're genuinely passionate about what you are doing. Otherwise it's going to feel like, "Why do I want to stay late when I could go out with my friends?" When you're much more interested in what you're doing than going out for a drink with friends, you've found your bliss.

# DAVID BOIES
# LAWYER

**I DIDN'T LEARN HOW TO READ UNTIL I WAS IN THE THIRD GRADE. BACK THEN, NOBODY I KNEW HAD EVER HEARD THE WORD "DYSLEXIA," BUT THAT'S WHAT I WAS EVENTUALLY** diagnosed as having. At the time, people just described me as "slow in reading." I was lucky because in the particular context I grew up in that was not a big deal.

It was the 1940s, and I lived in a small farming community in northern Illinois, where my father taught history and journalism at the local high school. Most of the graduates weren't intending to pursue professional or academic careers, and reading was certainly not a highly prized skill among first through sixth graders. We all had a variety of abilities, and the fact that I was not good at one of them didn't seem to matter that much. I couldn't jump very high either.

My dyslexia actually ended up benefiting me in an indirect way. It caused me to develop some useful skills. For example, public speaking. When I was thirteen, my family relocated to Southern California, and I signed up for the school debate team. While a lot of my team-mates referred to notes in the midst of a debate, my dyslexia prevented me from doing so. If I looked down at my notes, it would take me a while to figure out where I was and read what I had written. When you're speaking, even a pause that's only a few seconds long leaves an awful lot of awkward dead time. As a result, I learned to speak extemporaneously from an outline. This technique enabled me to maintain a certain naturalness that has proved to be very effective in communicating with judges, juries, and audiences in general.

Dyslexia also forced me to become a better listener. We all get some of our information from reading and some from listening. Because I had difficulty reading, I needed to depend

more on listening. When you really pay attention to the words people use, it tells you a great deal about what they mean and where they're going with what they're saying. If you hear a false note, for example, it tells you that they're avoiding something. The ability to listen to people has proved valuable, particularly when I'm cross-examining a hostile witness.

My grades in high school were okay, but because reading was difficult for me, I didn't particularly enjoy it. What I did enjoy was playing cards, drag racing, and partying with my girlfriend, Caryl. She was new to the school my junior year, and I fell in love with her immediately. It took me a week to make her my debate partner and a month to make her fall in love with me. At the end of my senior year, Caryl and I married.

When I graduated from high school, I had no intention of going to college. My goal was just to have a good time and make enough money to support my carefree lifestyle. And Caryl completely supported this game plan. I first worked on a construction crew then, when the weather got rainy, I got a job as a bookkeeper at a local bank. Construction work was hard and bookkeeping was boring, but Caryl and I were on our own, answering to no one but ourselves. I supplemented our income by playing cards, and we would spend our free time doing all the things young people do in Southern California: hanging at the beach, swimming, surfing, and taking the occasional drive down to Mexico. Things were idyllic. I had no sense that our lives would or should change.

But one day, about eight months after my graduation, we discovered that Caryl was pregnant. At first, she and I agreed that becoming parents wouldn't mean that we'd have to change our life, but a couple months before our baby was born, something shifted in Caryl and she became extraordinarily more responsible. She decided that it was time for me to make something of myself and that I should go back to school. Each day when I came home from work, a new school application or catalogue was there to greet me. Caryl would go on and on about how interesting the courses seemed and how nice the school looked.

I was hesitant. I knew that going back to school would be hard to manage financially and that I would have to compete academically with students who were better readers and more disciplined than I had ever been. But Caryl was determined. She felt I owed it to myself to try.

I was admitted to the University of Redlands in nearby San Bernardino County, and for the first time in my life grades were important. The university had given me a scholarship— my SAT scores were high—and I knew that in order to keep it I would have to perform well. I devoted more time to studying than ever before, and I also joined the debate team. Ironically, I think I was better prepared for college than I would have been had I gone directly after high school. I was more mature and had more motivation—having a child to support will do that to you.

I thought very seriously about becoming a high school history teacher like my father. But during the first semester of freshman year, I saw a sign-up sheet for the Law School

Admission Test, and I figured I should keep my options open and take it. If I hadn't signed up right then, I would probably never have gone to law school. I later discovered that law schools were accepting students after only three years of college. I calculated that if I increased my academic load and went to summer school I could finish three years of coursework in two. The notion of getting double credit for what would have been my senior year in college was too attractive to pass up, so law school it was.

I ended up going to Northwestern Law then transferring to Yale for my last year. Caryl and I had two children at this point; making ends meet wasn't easy. I always had to have a job on the side. Throughout my first year of law school, I worked as a night clerk in a motel from midnight to eight a.m. After this, I would head directly to class. On the strength of my first-year grades and professors' recommendations, I was eventually able to get a job at a law firm doing research.

Upon graduation, I was pretty certain that I wanted to become a law professor, but I thought it would be a good idea to get a little real-world experience first. I interviewed with several firms and got an offer from the New York firm Cravath, Swaine & Moore. Working in Manhattan was not a natural choice (I had never been east of Chicago until I went to Yale), but Cravath had such an excellent reputation that I couldn't refuse. I thought, *This will be for only a couple of years so why not?* Inertia's a powerful force. I ended up staying at Cravath for more than thirty years.

When a major Cravath client objected to my representing the New York Yankees, I left to start my own firm. It was a difficult decision that a lot of people feared I would regret. At Cravath I had enormous financial security. I had an entire army of secretaries, clerks, paralegals, and accountants helping me. At my new firm I was in a loft in Westchester County with one person helping out, and the Yankees were my only client. It was a risk, but one I understood well. I felt it would work out, and it has. Not only was it a good financial move, but I've also had the freedom to focus on cases that I'm truly passionate about. If you're a worrier or a second-guesser, making a major career change like this isn't going to work. You have to be able to move forward and live in the present.

My career has had its fair share of victories and failures. It's important not to be either too encouraged or too discouraged by what's happening at any particular moment. No matter what you do, there will be times when things go well and times when things go badly. The only thing for sure, in either scenario, is that things will change. When something good happens, I try to enjoy it. When something bad happens, I try to understand why it happened. But in either case, the next day I'm on to something else.

## DAVID'S PEARLS

■ In almost every major case that I've been in, and throughout my life, patience has served me well. To start, patience conserves time and energy. It is not true that a watched pot never boils, but it is true that a watched pot doesn't boil any faster because you're anxiously watching it. People who lack patience make all kinds of mistakes. Sometimes they'll tell you things they wish they hadn't because they just couldn't refrain from speaking. Sometimes they don't take the time to really know the facts and they say things that are incorrect. Sometimes they give up too early. I see that all the time: people not having the patience to stay with something that could have been successful. Before making a move, you should know as much as you can about your alternatives. Be clear about what you're trying to accomplish and how you're going to attempt it. Listen as much as you can before you speak. Give your opponent the opportunity to make the mistakes.

■ People see me in action at a trial and think I'm good at seizing moments extemporaneously—but what they don't see is the tremendous amount of work I've done to prepare. I can only take advantage of opportunities when they arise at trial because of all the time I've spent getting ready. I read thousands of pages of documents, interview people, research other cases, etc. It's tedious—like panning for gold. You have to wash away a lot of sand before finding a little nugget.

■ From the time I graduated high school through my years in law school, playing cards was a non-trivial part of what I did (and a non-trivial part of my income). Interestingly enough, it's also been a non-trivial source of useful lessons. Cards taught me a lot of what I know about patience. If you can avoid committing yourself until you've seen as many cards as possible, you'll make a better decision. Poker gave me some insight into how the human mind works. Bridge taught me about logic. Playing for money helped me learn about discipline and how to manage risk.

# JOHN PAUL DEJORIA

## JOHN PAUL MITCHELL SYSTEMS/PATRÓN SPIRITS COMPANY CO-FOUNDER

**I GREW UP IN DOWNTOWN LOS ANGELES. MY PARENTS DIVORCED WHEN I WAS TWO, AND FROM THAT POINT ON, IT WAS JUST MY MOTHER, MY BROTHER, AND I. WE HAD** almost no money. I remember a time when all we had was twenty-seven cents.

My mother assured us, "We are just fine. We have food in the refrigerator, we have our little garden around back, and next week more money will be coming in. We are actually rich because we are as happy as can be." She taught us that being rich and successful is a result of how happy you are and how well you do your job, not how much money you make.

As a kid, I thought it would be really cool to work so I could contribute to the family. I entered into my first entrepreneurial venture with my brother when I was seven years old. We would buy wood from the Variety Boys Club for twenty-five cents, use it to make flower boxes, then sell them for fifty cents each. We made a twenty-five-cent profit and thought it was amazing. At nine years old I sold Christmas cards, and when I was eleven I got my first morning paper route. To me, having a job was a privilege. My brother and I gave everything we earned to our mother so we could afford new sheets and things like that.

I graduated high school when I was seventeen. I didn't have the money to go to college, so I immediately enlisted in the United States Navy, where I remained on active duty for three years. When I got out, I worked a variety of jobs—from driving a tow truck to selling *Collier's Encyclopedia* door-to-door, which was a formative experience for me. If that job

existed today I would make every one of my kids do it. It was all cold-calling, convincing people to let me make a presentation. The goal was to get them, in an hour or less, to buy a set of encyclopedias for their family. I had to learn to overcome rejection, because after you've had fifteen doors slammed in your face, you need to be as enthusiastic at door number sixteen as you were at the first door if you want to make a sale. The average life of an encyclopedia salesman was three days, but I did it for three years! I was able to last so long because I truly believed that everyone needed a set of these books and that I was doing something good for my customers. If you don't believe in what you are selling, then you are just a salesman. I saw myself as somebody who helped people make the right decision. From there, I went on to vend everything from life insurance to medical linen to dictating equipment.

Eventually, when I was twenty-six, I got a job working at Time, Inc. as a circulation manager. I asked my boss what I had to do to become a vice president, and he said, "Well, you don't have a college degree, so come back and ask me when you are thirty-five." I knew I didn't want to tread water for nine years, so I went looking for another job. A friend of mine was an employment counselor and told me about Redken, a company in the beauty industry that was hiring salesmen. The pay wasn't very good, but he said, "There is no limit to where you can go in that industry." He was right! I took the job at Redken and moved up the ladder very fast. Within a year and a half, I was the national manager of two of their divisions (chain salons and scientific schools) and doing extremely well.

Both of my divisions grew every year, but one day the vice president of the company fired me. He said, "You and your team are messing up the way we run a corporation. You visit our businesses then immediately leave. You don't hang out with the regional managers enough." I said, "That's because we don't have to. We go in, do our job really well, then leave." I didn't want to socialize with them on the weekends. I was going to love-ins in Griffith Park instead. Apparently, I didn't fit into Redken's corporate picture.

I then went to work for Fermodyl Hair Care, training their management and sales force on how to sell. I was with them for one year, and during that time, the company grew from $8 million to $12 million in sales. But, once again, I was fired by the vice president for not fitting in. He said, "This company is run by people who are Jewish—and you are not. On the weekends you go to your love-ins or whatever you do with your biker friends, and you don't hang out with us." I couldn't believe my ears! Today that would be called discrimination. He added, "I don't really like you anyway, so you're fired." He was a pretty mean guy. I left, sales plummeted, and within a year the vice president and his top two guys got fired.

My next job was working for the Institute of Trichology as the vice president of sales and marketing. Because they didn't have a lot of money, I agreed to work for $3,000 a month plus six percent of any new sales I created. In about a year I tripled the company's sales—but, once again, I was fired. This time it was because I made too much money. One of the owners said, "We can get someone to do your job for about one-third of what you are making." His reasoning was as stupid as can be; I left and the company went downhill fast.

Tired of being at the mercy of others, I decided to go out on my own as a consultant for people who wanted to join the beauty industry. I was good at it, but my clients were such small companies that they were always behind on the paychecks. So that didn't last very long.

Around that time, in 1980, my friend Paul Mitchell (that was his hairdressing name, his real name was Cyril T. Mitchell) was having some real challenges financially while he was trying to get a product line off the ground. Unfortunately, the quality and marketing weren't there. I suggested we start a business together. We decided to create a line of hair-care products for professional stylists. The plan was that Paul would own thirty percent of the company, I'd own thirty percent, and a European investor who was going to contribute $500,000 would own forty percent.

Things weren't going well with my former wife, so the day the money from our investor was supposed to come in I gave her almost everything we had and moved out. With just a few hundred bucks in my pocket, I planned to withdraw some of the investor's money and check into a hotel. Paul was in a similarly precarious financial situation. Unfortunately, the investor changed his mind at the last minute and the money never came in.

I said to Paul, "What are we going to do? How much can you put toward this business?" He said, "I can only spare $350." I knew I needed a couple of hundred bucks to live off of, so I borrowed $350 from my mom to match Paul's contribution. John Paul Mitchell Systems was started with only $700.

Too proud to tell anyone about my situation, I moved into my car and figured out how to get by on two dollars and fifty cents a day. I would wake up in the morning and shower at the Griffith Park tennis courts. For breakfast I'd get the Trucker's Special at the Freeway Café: An egg, a piece of toast, and a piece of bacon or one sausage, plus your choice of coffee or orange juice, all for ninety-nine cents. I ate as late as possible because breakfast had to last me till four-thirty p.m. when Mexican restaurants like El Torito would begin their margarita specials. For ninety-nine cents you got a margarita plus all you can eat salsa, chicken wings, mini tostadas, and other little munchies. Twenty chicken wings later, with the salsa serving as my vegetable, I was full for the night. I would leave a quarter tip at each place. I was a big tipper!

I parked my car on Mulholland Drive because it was safe. After a couple of weeks, Joanna Pettet, an actress I had known from years past, walked by and saw me. She said, "You're living in your car?! I can't believe it! I have an extra room I can let you have for a couple of months to give you a helping hand." So I stayed with her. She was a good lady. I got some

business cards printed up for John Paul Mitchell Systems with her home phone number on it. When you called, you'd hear her English accent on the answering machine. I also got a post office box with a Universal City address for fifteen bucks. Little things like having a fancy address and someone else's voice on your outgoing message can make your business look a lot bigger and more official.

To start, Paul and I made a sample run of two shampoos and a conditioner. I relied on the skills I developed selling encyclopedias and went from beauty salon to beauty salon, cold-calling. To say the least, we didn't have enough money for advertising, but we felt we had a product so good that once people used it they would reorder and recommend it. That was our entire philosophy. We even said, "If you are not completely happy with our product line, we will take back every single bottle you have left and give you your money back." At least four out of every five salons we approached turned us down, but when one did buy our products, we would show them how to use them, how to market them, and how to make sales to their patrons. We helped our customers become successful.

It was literally hand-to-mouth for the first eighteen months to two years. By all business laws, we should have folded every day during that period but about two years in we were finally able to pay our bills on time and even had $4,000 in the bank. We were, like, "Oh, my God, we made it!" That was a huge turning point. From then on, business improved bit by bit. By the third year things really started taking off, and we've grown ever since.

In 1989 Paul Mitchell died, and I started another business, the Patrón Spirits Company, with my friend Martin Crowley. Martin had been spending some time in Mexico for a separate business that we had started the year prior. Before he headed down on one of his trips, I told him, "Bring me back a couple of bottles of tequila. Buy whatever the aristocrats drink." He returned with two plain-looking bottles of the smoothest stuff I had ever tasted. We figured that if we hired a master tequila distiller to make it even smoother and found a nicer way to package it, we could be onto something. It was very expensive to produce so to make the venture worthwhile we had to sell it for thirty-seven dollars a bottle, which was unheard of back then (the really good tequilas were going for about fourteen dollars a bottle and normal ones were at about five or six dollars per bottle). But we believed that the world was ready for a high-end product and we established the category "ultra premium tequila." We manufactured a thousand cases (twelve thousand bottles) to start. I figured that if no one bought it I would keep the tequila and for the next ten years everybody I knew would get a bottle on his or her birthday, christening, bar mitzvah, or any other kind of occasion you could think of.

Business was slow at first, but once people got over the shock of the price and tasted our product, they wanted more. Clint Eastwood put Patrón in his movie *In the Line of Fire*, and Wolfgang Puck turned all his friends on to it. At Paul Mitchell, we gave it free to people at events. And there are now more than two hundred songs that mention Patrón in their lyrics!

I have started so many businesses over the years, from diamonds to solar energy to manufacturing boats and pet supplies. The common thread among them is that they were each exciting to me at the time. The key is to be passionate about what you are doing—and then meticulous about the quality of what you produce.

You don't always know what you want to do in life, but you sure know when something isn't right. My advice is that once you realize you don't want to pursue something get out. The sooner you exit a situation that's not meant to be, the sooner you can move toward your ultimate destiny.

Throughout my twenties and up until the second year of John Paul Mitchell Systems, there were many nights that I couldn't sleep because I had no money to pay my bills. I remember feeling so down that I thought, *I could look up and see an ant crawling above me*. But I've come to realize that things that appear to be setbacks at the time often end up being for the best. For example, it would have been *impossible* for me to start John Paul Mitchell Systems had I not learned what I did and made the connections I did from every one of my prior beauty industry jobs. Each experience equipped me with something essential to my ultimate success and put me on a path where I could make a difference in the world. Whether it's helping the homeless find jobs in America, feeding needy people all over the world, or protecting our waterways, I wouldn't be in a position to do any of it had I not gone through some really rough patches.

## JOHN PAUL'S PEARLS

■ Success unshared is failure. If you've "made it" and don't help others out along the way—if you don't do something to make the planet a better place—you're not successful at all; you are a failure. But remember that you can't help everybody out. You have to focus and contribute in ways that you think are most beneficial.

My mom instilled this philosophy in me. She always encouraged my brother and me to do good. She had us give to the Salvation Army when we had no more than a dime and taught us that no matter how much someone has or doesn't have there is always somebody who is worse off.

■ The difference between successful people and unsuccessful people is that successful people do all the things unsuccessful people don't want to do. Most people don't want to work more than they have to. They do the minimum they are paid to do. That's not the way to get ahead. Always do the best you can, not the least you can get away with. When you do your job, even if its just cleaning an office, do it as if somebody you want to impress is watching your every step.

■ You don't have to be good at everything to be successful. Do what you do best and try to find others who can fill in by doing the things you are not good at. For instance, I am terrible at details—accounting especially, so I hire accountants to help me. This frees me up to focus on the things I do excel at and I can run a more efficient operation.

■ The biggest hurdle people face in almost any business is rejection. If you know this in advance and are mentally prepared for it, you'll have a much easier time staying upbeat and eventually succeeding.

# J. CRAIG VENTER, PhD
## SCIENTIST

**I WAS A HORRIBLE STUDENT UP THROUGH HIGH SCHOOL AND A BIT OF A TROUBLEMAKER. IN SEVENTH GRADE ONE OF MY GOOD FRIENDS WAS A MEMBER OF HELL'S ANGELS.**
He was sixteen or seventeen, but he had flunked and been held back so many times that we were in the same grade. We used to sit in the back of the class and throw spitballs at the teacher instead of paying attention.

I literally came within a half of a degree of flunking out of high school. I luckily got a D- instead of an F in one class (on account of an extra credit paper they had me write) so I graduated. I think they couldn't bear the idea of seeing me again the next year!

How well people do in school usually depends on their skill set. I'm not great at memorizing, and the education system I was in was definitely geared toward rote memorization and regurgitation. As a result, I just checked out. I'm much more of a processor and intuitive integrator of information, which is very effective in the right environment as I discovered later on.

My family wasn't in a great economic situation so, in contrast to children today who are either overscheduled or spoon-fed everything, I was just sent out to play. I would collect stray lumber from construction sites and build forts, carts, soapbox racers, and a multitude of different objects. In my teenage years I even built my own powerboat. The creative freedom I had growing up was very formative. I joke that I came out of the education system with my curiosity and imagination intact because I avoided the education system.

I happened to be athletic and was a high school swimming champion. As a result, I was offered a swimming scholarship to the University of Arizona—but I turned it down because

I wasn't sure what I wanted to do with my life. Swimming is an intense sport, and I knew I wasn't up for spending six hours a day training and competing for the next four years. I also wasn't ready for college academically. I wanted to go out and play instead.

After graduating in 1965, I moved to Southern California and took up surfing. To make money, I worked nights at a Sears, Roebuck & Company warehouse putting price tags on toys. I also was a night clerk, an airport fuel-truck driver, and a baggage handler. But the war in Vietnam soon caught up with me and, within several months, I was drafted into the army. My parents, who were both in the U.S. Marine Corps during World War II, convinced me to enlist in the navy instead.

The first thing they had us do in boot camp was take a battery of tests. Out of 36,000 young men, I scored the highest, much to my amazement. As a result, I was given the choice of going to whatever school I wanted. My main goal was to get an education that would at least enable me to have a trade when I got out, but the schools for electronics and nuclear engineering required extending one's enlistment for twice the length of the schooling. The last thing I wanted to do was serve longer than needed. The only school that didn't require an extension was the medical corpsman school. No one explained to me that the reason was because there was a high turnover and low survival rate.

By random assignment, I ended up in the infectious disease ward of a San Diego naval hospital. People would show up inflicted with malaria, tuberculosis, and hepatitis. I found myself in an environment that complemented my learning skills. It was on-the-job training. If I was shown something once, I could do it. With all the woodworking I had done in my youth, I knew I was physically and mechanically skilled, but I didn't realize that this would translate to drawing blood and doing liver biopsies! It was very rewarding to be good at something. For the first time in my life, I was a sponge and loved learning.

In the military you're basically allowed to do as much as you are able to do so—within a year, at only nineteen—I was put in charge of the entire infectious disease department and was teaching residents and interns how to do spinal taps and other complex procedures. I was later transferred to a hospital in Long Beach and put in charge of an emergency room. Corpsmen would come into the ER with injuries from drunken brawls, and I would sit there for hours suturing wounds and doing surgeries. I really enjoyed helping people.

After less than two years, the inevitable happened and I was transferred to Vietnam. Nothing prepares you for that kind of situation. Hundreds to thousands of guys my own age were being killed day in and day out. The worst part was that very few of us believed in what we were doing there. It was a depressing situation, and after about five months, it got to be overwhelming. I decided to get away from it all and end my life.

I went to the beach, got in the water, and started swimming out to sea. My plan was to keep going till I was exhausted then sink into the dark waters and oblivion. More than a mile out, I saw a venomous sea snake surface to breathe. I began to have doubts about what I was doing, but I continued on until I encountered a shark. I was instantaneously consumed with fear. All thoughts of dying departed, and I realized that I very much wanted to live. I wanted to live more than I ever had in the previous twenty-one years of my life. I turned around and, driven by sheer adrenaline, swam for the shore in a state of panic.

Once I made it to safety, I never looked back. Something inside me had changed. I wanted my life to mean something. I wanted to make a difference in the world. I wanted to do something to make up for everything I saw in Vietnam and honor those who were already beyond my help.

My original plan after the war was to get an MD degree then practice medicine in the third world. But to do that, I knew I would have to start from scratch given my poor educational history. As I was unable to spell even some of the most basic words, my only choice was to start at a community college—I would have to figure out how to learn in a classroom and study for the first time.

There were many guys in Vietnam who had similar experiences to mine but weren't able to get over the trauma and adapt to school when they got home. I, fortunately, had loads of motivation on my side. With the same skill set I had in high school combined with my new resolve, I was able to get all A's, and after two years, I transferred to the University of California, San Diego (UCSD).

As part of my undergraduate curriculum at UCSD, I encountered some very famous scientists who opened my eyes to a new world. Many people have huge delusions or are very misinformed about science. It's really just trying to answer questions about life that nobody knows the answer to. It's trying to figure out how things work so you can fix them. That's all. The possibilities piqued my curiosity, and I began to work with some of these scientists. I made some early breakthroughs and was both hooked (because it was one of the most gratifying things I'd ever done) and elated (because I had escaped the limitations of my early education). I realized that, as a physician, I could see maybe one hundred patients a day; but as a scientist, if I could come up with a breakthrough, I'd potentially be able to affect everyone on the planet. I had found my true calling and decided to pursue science instead of medicine.

I got both my bachelor's degree and PhD from UCSD and then went on to work as a professor at SUNY Buffalo and the Roswell Park Cancer Institute. In 1984 I was recruited by the National Institutes of Health (NIH), the powerhouse of medical research in America. Accepting that offer changed my life and the course of my science. It was at NIH that I became passionate about the power of genomics to radically transform health care, and I joined the government-funded Human Genome Project.

The goal of this program, as the name implies, was to sequence the human genome. What does this mean? Your genome is the complete set of your genetic information.

Everything you inherited from your parents, everything they inherited from their parents, and so on (back through the history of humanity) is contained in six billion chemical letters written in DNA code. Sequencing a human genome means reading all six billion letters to figure out what they have to say. It was such a lofty goal that most people thought it would be impossible. But the medical possibilities that this information can lead to are endless. For example, knowing which genes a person has can tell us how likely he is to develop various diseases. And if someone already has a disease, knowing which genes he has can tell us which drugs have the best chance to cure him.

I was part of NIH's program for about nine years but became frustrated with how slowly things were moving. We had been using a method called "shotgun sequencing" to sequence small pieces of DNA. My team and I believed that this method would be the fastest and most effective way to sequence the whole human genome. We applied for a grant to explore it further, but our request was denied. The government thought that using shotgun sequencing to sequence the whole human genome would be impossible. The lumbering government bureaucracy was locked into its way of doing things and didn't want to try anything new.

I wanted to go off on my own and have the freedom to do research my way. The problem was that this would require major funding. But in 1992 I found an investor who was willing to put up to $70 million for me to start my own research institute in exchange for sharing my findings with his biotech company (so it could potentially profit from the information). This got things going on the right track, and in 1995 my team and I had a huge breakthrough by using shotgun sequencing to chart the whole genome of a free-living organism, the bacterium *Haemophilus influenzae*. Sequencing the *human* genome, however, was still a lot more complex, and the money required to do so was at a different level altogether.

I eventually found a company that was willing to put up the money required to get things going—$300 million—but unfortunately they wouldn't allow me to do the experiments at my institute. The catch this time was that I had to partner with them and start a for-profit corporation.

In 1998 we founded Celera Genomics and announced to the world that, using whole-genome shotgun sequencing, we would successfully sequence the human genome years earlier, and for less money, than the government-sponsored Human Genome Project. It was one of the most intense and challenging periods of my life. Celera soon became a public company, and I had to learn how to raise money for it on Wall Street while doing science that nobody thought was possible—all the while being severely attacked by the government-funded program scientists.

You see, what we were doing at Celera was a major threat to the government's five-billion-dollar public program. The people leading that effort thought they were the only ones in the game and were therefore guaranteed fame and fortune. Next thing they knew, an upstart was threatening to do in one year what they planned on taking well over a decade to complete. They harshly criticized the validity of using shotgun sequencing for the task and attacked me personally. But fortunately, as far as science is concerned, the presence of a competitor lit a fire under the government program and caused them to perform better than they would have otherwise.

The amazing thing is that we were able to sequence the human genome in just nine months. Even though we were way ahead of the government's effort, I decided to declare a draw and announce our breakthrough with them and the President of the United States. Although on some level it would have been very satisfying to defeat them after all of their attacks, in the end I decided that doing this wasn't good for me, my team, or anyone. Science is about changing humanity and changing medicine—not about who wins, loses, or gets credit. I thought it was important to get that into perspective and set a good example for generations to come.

Although it will take decades to completely understand everything that the reading of DNA reveals, our breakthrough changed what's happening across the board in medicine. Every new medical development now uses human gene information as its foundation, and shotgun sequencing is now the method used by its earlier critics.

After our big breakthrough, the people on the business end of Celera became very focused on turning it into a pharmaceutical company. I remained focused on going further with my scientific research. One day I mentioned to a Celera board member that I was thinking of going back to my own institute. Two days later I was fired. They were worried that if word got out that I was going to leave it would hurt the stock. I wanted to leave, but because of the abrupt change—I didn't even have the opportunity to say good-bye to my team—it was probably one of the toughest times I've been through. I went from dealing with the world press every day and having all these people report to me to nothing. In an instant my main identity was pulled away, and I was back to being just me. I was shocked at how utterly lost I felt. It took a few months to adapt. I went sailing around the Caribbean and thought about what I wanted to do. Many people would have been happy to quit at that point. But I still had a lot I wanted to accomplish. So I came back and started a new institute and a company called Synthetic Genomics.

Now I'm working on the creation of synthetic life, which is as important, if not more so, than sequencing the human genome. This breakthrough has many applications for the future. By synthetically making DNA, we can now make a flu vaccine in a few hours instead of the nine months it used to take. We're also using the technology to make new sources of medicine and energy and to create new food types.

Along with Synthetic Genomics, I also recently started another company, Human Longevity Inc., which is dedicated to using advances in genomics along with stem-cell therapeutics to extend and enhance the healthy human life span. I think my best work is yet to come.

## CRAIG'S PEARLS

■  Success in any field is largely about taking risks. While I have always been somewhat of a risk taker, my time in Vietnam really helped put things in perspective. Out there I had to worry about losing my life multiple times a day. Being back in the comfort of America with my life relatively protected, career risks seemed pretty trivial. As a result, I've gone out on professional limbs that very few people would. My government job with NIH provided me with guaranteed employment and science funding, but I gave all that up to pursue what most of my peers viewed as a real long shot. My sequencing experiment could have failed, and I would have been left without a source of income, but I believed so strongly that my method would work that I was willing to take the risk.

■  The biggest obstacle I continually face is the static resistance to new ideas and new approaches. If you look at the history of breakthroughs in science and medicine, almost everything that's turned out to be a major development was initially attacked by the establishment—mainly because it was a threat. Thomas Kuhn wrote about the stages of paradigm shifts in his book, *The Structure of Scientific Revolutions*: First a new idea is attacked then it's reluctantly accepted. Along with the acceptance comes denial that it was ever an issue to begin with and a bit of historical revision that it was never that big of a breakthrough. A great example of this can be seen through the story of Barry Marshall, the Australian physician who discovered that bacteria causes stomach ulcers. At the time of Marshall's breakthrough, the whole medical establishment believed that ulcers were caused by stress, spicy foods, and too much acid. In addition, the whole pharmaceutical industry was based on this premise (antacids were sold to treat stomach ulcers). The last thing they wanted the cause of ulcers to be was bacteria—so Marshall and his theory were severely attacked over and over again. Finally in 1984, he drank a whole petri dish of bacteria to prove his point. He developed severe ulcers, and it was slowly accepted that bacteria was the cause of not only stomach ulcers but also of stomach cancer. Marshall finally received the Nobel Prize in 2005 for his discovery, but it was only through that kind of perseverance that he was able to prove his point and overcome the opposition.

This phenomenon, unfortunately, is not unique to science. Life is about competition. Certain people intensely dislike others because they're either successful or do things differently. Politicians get this all the time for picking one party over another. It's discouraging that people work at this basic level, but that's part of humanity. You really need to believe in yourself and not let others' opinions define you.

■ Being able to change directions when needed is essential in life, especially in science. Sometimes you go down a dead-end path, but that's part of the process. The sooner you realize it the better so you can get on the right track. Most scientists work in a linear fashion. They'll spend years doing something, and then do the final experiment, which won't work because their theory was flawed from the beginning.

I like to start with quick and dirty experiments to gauge if we are on the right track. If we are, I get intensely focused and put 110 percent into proving it and making it work in an elegant fashion. When we're not, we reassess and change directions. My team will tell you that I reserve the right to change my mind and that I'm constantly rethinking things. It's like sailing. The way you go upwind is to tack back and forth from one side to another and slowly work your way up. You can't go straight into the wind.

■ Ideally, I wish I had started my formal education earlier—it would have given me more time to accomplish the things I want to in life. However, my real-world education was necessary to shape me into the person I am. I hope that others won't need to experience anything close to the intensity of war to find themselves, but I see more and more kids taking off for a year or so after they finish college and doing something different. I think that's smart if you don't know what you want to do and can afford the time. So many people get pushed along in the "system," and because they don't really know what they want to do, they practically let their careers be chosen for them. If you're not passionate about what you're doing, it's hard to be successful at it. You can show up and do what's required, and you can even do your job well, but that's not where real success is going to come from. Success comes from doing something extraordinary with passion and intensity.

■ A key element to my success has been my ability to attract the best people in the world to work with me—and then keep them motivated. A lot of scientists isolate themselves in their laboratories. To me, science is about team building. I work with large multidisciplinary teams composed of physicists, mathematicians, biochemists, biologists, and computer scientists. We all intermingle in a shared workspace and contribute our own personal expertise to solve a problem. I've found that most people like being part of something larger than themselves and accomplishing an ambitious goal.

# LESLIE MOONVES
## CBS PRESIDENT AND CEO

**I NEVER LIKED A DAY OF SCHOOL IN MY LIFE. BE IT ELEMENTARY SCHOOL, HIGH SCHOOL, OR COLLEGE—IT DIDN'T MATTER. I WAS ALWAYS BORED AND COULDN'T WAIT** until class was over. To me, it was all just a means to an end. I attended Bucknell University and was initially premed, but that was only because I didn't have a strong interest in anything else. Plus, it made my parents very happy.

Before long, I realized that the sciences and I were not made for each other. Talk about not being interested! So I gave that up, went off to Europe, and spent my junior year at the University of Madrid. I had a great time, but I still had no idea what I wanted to do with my life.

Upon returning to Bucknell as a senior, I had to pick a major. Because I had just spent a year accruing Spanish credits, I selected Spanish. But I also became active in the theater department that year. An extraordinary professor named Harvey Powers ran the program and was an inspiration to me. He thought I had a talent for acting and suggested a few graduate schools. I followed his advice and got accepted to a two-year program at the Neighborhood Playhouse in New York. It was, and still is, probably the best acting school in the country.

From there, I ventured into the world of professional acting and started to get some work. Most of it was guest-star spots on television shows. Although the roles sometimes got a little bigger, I was never immensely successful and had to tend bar at night to pay my bills. The life of a partially employed actor created a lot of tension because it wasn't stable. I had to wait around for auditions to come my way. I couldn't plan my life. I couldn't plan on going on vacation. I couldn't plan on a steady stream of income. My hand was always out—as if I were saying, "Please like me!" I did not feel in control.

At a certain point I looked around and realized that despite my amazing training I was never going to be a great actor. I observed my contemporaries and realized that many of them had a lot more talent than I did. I was mediocre at best. My teacher at the Neighborhood Playhouse, Sandy Meisner, once said something that really stuck with me. He said, "You should only be an actor if acting is the only thing you can do." I realized that that wasn't me.

A friend of mine, the actor Gregory Harrison, had started a small production company, and we decided to produce a play together. The play was good, but it became way more successful than we had imagined because of a fluke. Our play was being performed in a tiny theater in Hollywood. One day, the man running the Ahmanson Theatre, the biggest theater in LA, came to see it because he was a friend of one of the other producers. He happened to come the day Natalie Wood drowned—and Natalie was supposed to star in the next production at the Ahmanson. So he took our little play instead and moved it from our ninety-nine-seat theater to his three-thousand-seat theater! It was a tremendous break. It was my first big paycheck and it enabled me to buy my first house.

At that point I left acting behind and moved forward producing theater. I realized I had strong organizational skills and was a good leader. I loved getting up in the morning, being busy with creative stuff, and feeling productive. It gave me a stable income and a stable life. I felt like I could control my own success. The harder I worked, the more successful I became. I was greatly relieved.

It's difficult to specifically map out your career. Things sometimes come at you and hit you in the face. If your path is rigid, you'll likely miss out on opportunities. You have to be fluid and open to change. I shifted from acting to producing theater and realized it felt great. Before long, I shifted again and got my first job in TV as a development executive at Columbia Pictures Television. That felt great too.

In contrast to my disinterest in school, I was a passionate student of the television industry. My goal was to figure out the game and how to win. I was like a sponge. I asked questions, talked to everybody I could, and spent a lot of time trying to figure out which executives were smart and which ones weren't.

One way to learn is through observing great mentors, but it's perhaps more valuable to learn by observing people with important jobs who you think are doing it wrong. In other words, you can gain a lot by looking at a person and thinking, *If I had that problem, I wouldn't do it that way.* There are more mediocre executives out there than good ones, so you can pick up a lot by just keeping your eyes open.

Ironically, one of the reasons people say I've done well in television is because I am easily bored. I constantly say, "Keep me entertained!" and I think that helps me find good content. My experience as an actor has also provided me with an advantage over some of my competitors. I know what it's like to audition, and I'm still very involved in casting a lot of our projects. I'm impressed by good acting and love that part of my job.

What may surprise some people, because I know I have a reputation for being kind of cocky, is that as a young executive I was pretty insecure and underestimated my capabilities. As I moved up the ranks, I always expected there to be greatness from my colleagues at each new level. I worried that I might not measure up. But when I got there, I usually realized that my new contemporaries were not as untouchable as I had imagined them to be and that I could catch onto things pretty quickly. The lesson is: don't automatically be intimidated by people who have achieved more professional success than you, and don't let your own insecurity bog you down. Move upward if you have the opportunity. Once you have the chance to survey the lay of the land, things are often not as hard to tackle as you might have imagined, and the people you assumed were so smart might not be.

When I was hired as president and CEO of CBS in 1995, the network was in last place and there was a loser mentality among the employees—which I hated. It was especially difficult for me because I had just come from Warner Bros. Television, where we were the number one studio and I was leaving a group of people that I really liked. For the first eighteen months, it wasn't fun getting up in the morning. It was a really difficult time. The main problem was that I was not surrounded by a great team, so we had to make a lot of changes. We wanted to hire a bunch of fresh, talented employees—people with good character who wanted to win—to replace those who were not working out with the company. There was a lot that went into it, and it was hard work every step of the way, but as a team we were eventually able to turn the ship around and bring the network from last to first place.

I am a big proponent of teamwork. Certain companies operate on a system of people trying to outdo or compete with one another. I don't believe in that. We win together (no one person gets all the credit) and we lose together (no one person gets all the blame). There are about 150 people involved with every television series we do. Some shows end up being hits, but two out of three fail. It's awesome when you have a hit, but when you have a failure with great people, you have to make them feel good about working with you again. And you can do that with the team theory: "It's not your fault. We win as a team, we lose as a team." And it's true—it takes a team to put on a show. By the way, people who are not team players don't understand that by not supporting the team—by looking for self-aggrandizement instead—they're only going to hurt themselves.

How you handle those around you is key to how you get ahead. If I find someone good, I try to hang on to him or her. It's essential to let employees feel secure about their jobs. Some companies don't, and the employees work out of fear and are constantly watching their backs. When my employees drive to work in the morning, I want them thinking 100 percent about their jobs and not about whether the guy in the next office is going to screw them or

whether they are going to be fired. That leads to nonproductivity. If people feel secure where they work, their performance is so much better.

I'm someone who assumes that what can go wrong will. In my business we can only control fifty percent of what we do—so it's imperative that we look ahead, identify possible pitfalls, and work our butts off to control what we can. That doesn't mean that things won't go wrong, but if I know I've done everything I could, then I don't feel as bad if they do (also, it makes our chances of success that much greater). I hate self-inflicted wounds. They bother me a lot.

## LESLIE'S PEARLS

■   If you want to pursue a career in my industry, get in the door any way you can and then do the best you can at that job, even if it's sweeping the floor of a production office. If you do the best job you can, somebody will notice, and opportunity will present itself. Let people see that you are willing to do anything and that you have a good attitude. When I walk down the halls, I notice people who are upbeat. The number one thing is to let others think of you as a "can-do" person. My daughter Sara is like that. I could tell her, "I need an elephant on my lawn at six tomorrow morning," and she'll have it there. No questions asked. Those are the kind of people who get ahead, the kind who don't necessarily ask questions but instead find solutions.

■   When you have to say no, do it nicely. We get pitched about five hundred television shows a year and only put four new ones on the air—so there's a tremendous amount of rejection going on—but we want those same people to come back to us when they have a hit show. If you're a creator, a writer, or a producer who's spent a year working on a TV show, it's your baby. You don't want to hear someone say, "Your baby's ugly." You want to hear something more sensitive like "Okay, it didn't work out this time, but if you do it in the right way, maybe next time." There are ways to get a clear message across without unnecessarily hurting feelings and burning bridges.

# JILLIAN MICHAELS
# FITNESS EXPERT

**YOU KNOW HOW CERTAIN PEOPLE CAN EAT WHATEVER THEY WANT AND NEVER GAIN A POUND? I'M NOT ONE OF THEM. I NEVER WAS. I WAS A CHUBBY KID. MY DAD IS** overweight, and I think I inherited my "fat gene" from him. We had a strained relationship and often bonded over food. When we were alone and had nothing to say to each other, it would be, like, "Let's go eat burritos!"

My mother is naturally thin, but she didn't know much about nutrition, so my diet consisted primarily of processed garbage like microwave mac 'n' cheese, or baloney on white bread with mayo, and Cheetos.

I grew up in Los Angeles. My parents got divorced when I was twelve years old and the upheaval took a heavy emotional toll on me. As I shuttled back and forth between their two homes, food became a great source of comfort. It was something stable that I could always look forward to. I was an only child until I was fifteen and a half, so I was lonely a lot. When I was having a tough day, I would think, *I'm going to order a large Domino's pizza, sit on the roof, and eat the whole thing by myself.*

By the time I was thirteen, I was approximately five feet tall and tipped the scale at 175 pounds. I had a nose the size of a softball (which I've since had fixed), a unibrow (had that fixed too!), braces, and acne. I was tormented at school. Kids made horse and cow sounds when I walked by and wrote nasty things on my locker. Once, I was surrounded by a group of kids and bullied about my weight, the size of my nose, and the fact that I was gay— which I didn't even know at the time. Things got so bad that my mom pulled me out of that school and enrolled me in another one for eighth grade. My new school wasn't much of an

improvement. I ate lunch with my teacher in her classroom every day because it was such hell on the schoolyard. I felt helpless and began acting out. I skipped classes and my grades plummeted. I started shoplifting. I was destructive at home and unruly.

Although I was in therapy, my mom felt I also needed a physical outlet. When I was thirteen, she enrolled me in a martial-arts class. I would show up and do my best, but I didn't really take the message to heart—I often showed up with a bag of chips and a soda in my hands. One day my instructor gave me an ultimatum. He said, "Don't waste my time. If you are not going to take this seriously, get out." It was a real wake-up call. I started to focus and began taking better care of myself. I was in an environment where people were supportive, and I admired the way they lived. They were ambitious, and their bodies were their temples. I wanted to be like them. To a large extent, you become the company you keep.

A major turning point occurred when I was just fourteen and took my second-degree blue belt test. I broke two boards with a side kick and was beyond proud. I wasn't better looking or even thinner at this point, but when I showed up for school the next day, I carried myself differently. I valued and respected myself. No one ever picked on me again. From then on, not only did I take my martial arts more seriously, but I also realized that when you feel strong physically it transcends into other facets of your life.

When I was seventeen, I graduated high school and my father threw me out of the house. He was domineering and our relationship had grown increasingly combative. My dad was wealthy, but he always made it clear to me that what we had was his, not mine. I ended up crashing in a studio apartment with a friend. My mother helped me pay rent until I was eighteen. For the most part, I've been supporting myself ever since. I enrolled at California State University, Northridge but dropped out after a year and a half. I've always had severe ADHD and was never a good student.

Around this time, I stumbled into training. I was at the gym, practicing for my black belt, when someone approached and asked if I was a trainer. I was, like, "How much does it pay?" I began to train during the day and bartend at night—yes, of course I blew fire and flipped bottles. Soon I was making more than $100,000 a year and loving life. Both jobs were really fun and social. I thought that someday I would open up a bar or a gym—or both—and continue to be happy for the rest of my life. I didn't know there was another goal.

But when I was twenty-three, I started dating someone in the entertainment industry and things changed. He was a thirty-year-old Ivy League graduate and he hung out with a group of friends who all had similar credentials. All of a sudden, I felt judged for being a trainer and bartender. What I had thought was the coolest career ever suddenly wasn't cool at all. I started to become ashamed of myself and I decided to switch careers.

I got a job as an assistant at a big talent agency. It took me several years, but I worked my way up the ladder and became an agent. I finally had a grown-up job with some clout, but I was miserable. I did not like my boss and I was hardly making enough money to pay my bills. I kept thinking, *This sucks, but I guess it's what I'm supposed to do.* I didn't know any better.

My boss wasn't the greatest guy and he had done something unethical. Since I had been his assistant, I knew about it and got pressured by another agent to disclose my information. In the end, the agency used the info to leverage my boss into renegotiating his contract, and I was fired.

So there I was at age twenty-seven without a clue as to what I was going to do with my life and feeling like I had just wasted four years of it. It was an extremely tough time. I literally could not get off the couch for months. It was so bad my mother thought I needed to be on antidepressants so I took Zoloft for about four months (and I am *not* into medication). I was so numbed out that it was only when my car got towed and I found this to be hilarious that I knew I needed to get off of it.

Eventually, after an exhausting job search that turned up nothing, a friend of mine who was running a sports medicine facility suggested I work for her as a physical therapy aid and trainer. At first, I found the notion humiliating—it would be taking a huge step backward on my career path—but I had to pay my bills so I didn't really have a choice. The interesting thing is that I soon found myself waking up in the morning looking forward to work. I adored my clients and really cared about how they progressed. One day I got a call from a very overweight woman I had been working with. She tearfully said, "I felt my hip bone for the first time in eight years and I just wanted to thank you." I started to cry hysterically. At that moment I realized, *This is what I'm supposed to do. I'm where I'm meant to be.* I loved my life again.

For me, what I do is not about fitness. It's about helping people rebuild their lives. Fitness is just the tool I use to empower them. By helping people feel healthy, strong, and capable, I'm able to redefine their entire self-image and transform years of negativity. I'm able to do for them what martial arts did for me years ago.

I eventually decided to open my own sports medicine facility with the help of some of my clients who became angel investors. I had a podiatrist, a chiropractor, and a physical therapist all working for me, but I also worked under and learned from them. This was an incredibly happy time in my life. I was in charge of my own destiny and doing what I loved. This went on until I was about thirty when I was selected to be a trainer on the reality TV show *The Biggest Loser.*

An agent I had become friends with while working at ICM had heard about the show and recommended that they hire me. So, as it turned out, my stint in the entertainment industry wasn't a waste of time after all!

The rest is history. I've been able to use my visibility from the show to develop a brand name for myself and build a health and wellness empire that includes *New York Times* best-selling books, fitness DVDs, video games, clothing, apps, websites, and more.

But not every venture I've embarked on since *The Biggest Loser* has been a success. In 2010, for example, I did my own reality TV show called *Losing It with Jillian*. I would live with an overweight family for a week and change their eating and exercise habits. After six weeks on their own, I would return to see how they progressed. The show failed. We were giving people who were three to four hundred pounds six weeks to lose weight. Even if they lost fifty pounds, they still looked almost exactly the same. I kind of knew this would be a problem before I even signed on, but I did the show because others thought I should and because I was afraid that I might never get another comparable opportunity.

I believe that every failure, disaster, and heartbreak has a silver lining. *Losing It* was a professional disaster, but I got two great things out of it. First, I learned this simple but important lesson: If your gut tells you something's wrong, don't do it. And, second, I discovered the joy of parenting. One of the families I lived with had a nine-year-old girl I really bonded with. Spending time with her made me realize for the first time that I wanted kids of my own. I now have two children and am more fulfilled than ever.

## JILLIAN'S PEARLS

■   In every business and in every facet of life there are "gatekeepers." Gatekeepers are people who decide whether or not you get past them to do what you want to do. If they won't let you pass via the traditional route, your job is to get around them in whatever way you can. For example, if you want to sell a product and can't get a retailer to take it, sell it yourself on the Internet. If you have a message you want to get across but can't get your own TV show, put your material on YouTube or iTunes. Play by your own set of rules and defeat the naysayers and gatekeepers by forging your own path to success. The only way you are ever going to get where you want is to keep moving in that direction. I think Gloria Steinem said it best: "Whatever it is that you want to do, just do it."

■   No one likes to feel vulnerable, and I'm no exception, but the reality is that you can only know as much depth, happiness, and success in your life as you can know vulnerability. If you don't ask out a girl or a guy on a date, you won't get rejected, but you won't fall in love either. If you don't apply for the job, then you won't get the position you want. If you don't try to start your own business, then you'll never be the entrepreneur you always dreamed of being.

# JIM KOCH
# BREWER AND FOUNDER OF THE BOSTON BEER COMPANY

**EVEN THOUGH EVERY ELDEST SON IN MY FAMILY SINCE THE 1840s HAS BEEN A BREWMASTER, NO ONE COULD HAVE PREDICTED THAT I WAS DESTINED TO BECOME ONE** as well. Not with the way the industry had evolved, not with the little guys getting squeezed out by the big mass-produced brands. In the last six months of my father's brewing career, he made a total of $500.

He had four kids and was hardly getting by. Wanting more for me, my father did everything he could to discourage me from honoring my legacy and following in his footsteps. He urged me to get good grades so I could open new doors. I fulfilled his dream by not only getting into Harvard's undergraduate program but also, later, an elite program there that allowed me to complete both law and business school simultaneously.

I mostly enjoyed college, but I found grad school ungratifying. It was during my second year, when the pressure was on to find a summer job, that I had an epiphany. None of the conventional career paths excited me. I thought, *I'm twenty-four years old and have never done anything but go to school. I now have to make incredibly important choices, but I don't have a basis of experience to make them.* I felt as if I were on an airplane headed somewhere I didn't like and had to parachute. So I headed to Colorado where I found my calling as an Outward Bound instructor. It was a great fit. Already heavily into mountaineering, I spent three and a half years living and climbing everywhere from crags outside Seattle to volcanoes in Mexico.

Eventually, there came a day when I was ready to return and complete my law and business programs at Harvard. Upon graduation, I landed a high-paying job at the Boston

Consulting Group. But while that seemed like success to most people, I eventually found myself asking, "Is this really what I want to be doing when I'm fifty?"

After about five years at BCG, I had my second epiphany. The idea came to me one weekend while I was helping my dad clean out his attic. We found an old trunk containing some beer recipes scrawled on scraps of yellowing paper. Looking at them with nostalgia, he told me, "Today's beer is basically water that can hold a head." I agreed. If you didn't want to drink the mass-produced American stuff, the only other choices at the time were imports that were often either stale or skunky. I remember thinking, *Americans pay good money for inferior beer. Why can't I make a good beer for Americans right here in America?*

Everybody, *especially* my father, thought it was a dumb idea. At the time, there were no "microbrewery" success stories out there and nobody was making a living from it. In other words, it was in no way, shape, or form a promising industry.

I had learned some great life lessons from mountaineering that helped me move forward. One of them relates to how climbers differentiate between objective and subjective risks. An objective risk is something that can kill you. A subjective risk is something that just frightens you. The two are often extremely different, but, unfortunately, things that frighten you are often not the real dangers, and the real dangers are often things that don't frighten you. As a result, our instincts don't always work effectively.

For example, my Outward Bound students were always scared of the rappelling portion of the trip. And I understand why—they had to stand at the edge of a 150-foot cliff and walk off it backward with only this little rope in their hands. I constantly had to talk them into it. But while that seems like a very risky thing to do, it's not. Those ropes will hold a car. Nobody ever gets killed doing that. On the other hand, walking up a not-so-steep glacier with nice, bright sun on a beautiful May morning, *that's dangerous.* Because it's May, the snow is melting. Underneath are all these layers put down during the winter. On some of them it snowed and then there was a little rain and then it iced and then, perhaps, some soft snow fell on top of that. That's a very unstable combination. It avalanches. Avalanches don't often happen on the steep, scary-looking slopes. The snow doesn't accumulate enough on those steep inclines. It's the gentler slopes that can kill you.

While I was still pondering my beer idea, I had a conversation with one of my mentors— a senior guy at General Electric. I mentioned the risk involved and he said something very insightful: "Jim, I would sooner hire you for a senior position at General Electric with two years of failed entrepreneurship on your résumé than with two more years at BCG." He didn't think that trying something entrepreneurial was an objective risk because I'd always be able to rejoin the work force if it didn't work out. It *seemed* like a risky thing to do because it looked very likely to fail, but the real risk was *not* doing it. The objective risk was wasting years of my life stuck in something that appeared attractive but that I really didn't enjoy. A lot of entrepreneurship and innovation seems perilous, but it's not. And a lot of things that seem safe and comfortable are, in fact, profoundly risky. *That's* subjective versus objective risk.

So I took the leap and set out to raise money for a brewery. Although I tried my hardest, I couldn't get bank loans or venture money, but what was most interesting to me was that none of the most senior people at BCG wanted to invest. None of the allegedly "smartest business minds out there" thought my idea had an upside. They were probably right, at least at the time. But I got friends, relatives, and a client or two to put their money with me.

I learned another obvious lesson from mountaineering: You never climb a mountain to get to the middle; you climb it to get to the top. So I set our company's goal as becoming the largest and most respected high-end beer in the United States. That was the summit for us. At the time, the company was made up of two people (me and my former BCG assistant, Rhonda), so it was an insane goal. But I couldn't see any other reason to climb the mountain.

It wasn't exactly smooth sailing. I figured that once the beer was made I could hire somebody else to sell it for me (by law, beer has to go from a brewer to a wholesaler to a retailer to a consumer), but I couldn't even get a wholesaler to represent me! There were five in Boston at the time and they all turned me down. "Your beer is too expensive, nobody knows you, and people won't drink expensive American beer, no matter how good it is. They want imported beer." That's what I heard across the board. I solved the problem by getting my own wholesaler's license, leasing a truck, and cold-calling the bars myself. It's funny looking back on it now. Not knowing any better, I lined my fancy leather briefcase with ice packs, filled it with beer, and hit the bars in my best suit.

People tend to think way too linearly about career paths, but career wanderings often have great outcomes too. There's a whole lot less urgency than you think. It's okay to drop out, breathe, and try other stuff. I could not have designed a better life's work. I get up every morning excited. I am completely fulfilled and have not gotten the least bit bored or tired, which is unusual. But the path didn't appear to me until I was thirty-four, and my wanderings are what prepared me for it.

I have an old message from a guy framed and hung on my office wall. It says: "I'll call back on Monday." It was a Friday when he called and left that message with my secretary. On Sunday night, the guy died of a heart attack. He was only thirty-four. Monday never came. *Monday doesn't always come.* Whether "Monday" is ten years from now or tomorrow, you may not have the chance to do the things you say you will sometime down the road. Think about the things you want to do with your life and try to get them done. Particularly when you are young. There are a lot of things that if you don't do them in your twenties you'll never do. Make sure you get the important experiences out of the way early, because once you start a career, get married, and have a family, you probably won't have a large chunk of time off for the next thirty years.

## JIM'S PEARLS

- A lot of businesses become successful because they have a superior product and a founder who is passionate about it. But frequently, as the company grows and the founder's job expands, the quality of the product is forgotten. Never take your eyes off of your product! If anything, as your company makes more money, use those resources to *improve* your product. I still personally taste and approve every single batch of beer that we send out. And a glass of Sam Adams Boston Lager today is noticeably better than it was when we started because I can now afford to invest in things like better ingredients and more sophisticated equipment.

- The Boston Beer Company has a simple hiring standard—never hire someone unless they will raise the average. Before we employ anyone, we ask, "Is this person better than the average of the current people we have working in this position?" If the answer is no, we don't make the hire. When you bring someone on board who is below your company's average, you degrade the quality of your company. If you always hire people who raise your average, your company gets increasingly better. We sometimes spend an insanely long time searching for someone to fill a spot. I think our record is eighteen months (for a sales position in Arizona), but it's now fifteen years later and the woman we hired is still with us. The payoff was definitely worth it.

# IAN SCHRAGER
# ENTREPRENEUR/ HOTELIER/REAL ESTATE DEVELOPER

**I GREW UP IN BROOKLYN. BACK THEN IT WAS VERY MIDDLE CLASS AND EVERYONE WAS STRIVING TO IMPROVE THEIR LOT IN LIFE. I'M HAPPY I WASN'T RAISED SOMEWHERE** more affluent. I think it made me hungrier. I had no idea where I was going or what road I would travel on, but I knew I wanted to be successful.

I have always been very competitive and driven, in sports or whatever. I think that's a quality you either have or you don't. In the end, there's so little that separates people. Those who want success the most and are relentless about pursuing it are the ones who get it.

I realize now that it's practically impossible to know what you want to do when you start out. For most people, it's usually a process of experimentation and elimination. I went to Syracuse University and majored in economics, and then went on to law school—not because I really wanted to practice law but because I wasn't sure what I wanted to do. I figured that wherever I landed, being a lawyer and learning how to think analytically would be beneficial. I ended up practicing law for about three years. One day a friend asked, "Why would you want to advise people who are out there doing things instead of doing them on your own?" That really resonated with me. I decided I wanted to do something entrepreneurial and partnered with my college friend, Steve Rubell. We chose to go into the nightclub business, in large part because there were very few barriers to entry—it didn't require a tremendous amount of capital and there wasn't a huge learning curve.

I don't follow the adage that it's not good to do business with friends. I think it is good. It's nice to share success with a friend, and a friendship can help resolve difficulties that might arise. But it's important to choose a partner who complements your skill set rather than

someone who excels at the same things you do. Steve and I were perfect together for that reason.

I've always been shy. It is very difficult for me to make aimless banter, and I'm not very interested in socializing. I suppose there's a contradiction in possessing those qualities and being in the hospitality business, but as a result, I've always relied on the strength of my work to carry the day. I am creative and there isn't a detail that I'm not interested in. Steve, on the other hand, was extremely social. He loved the people, the visibility, and the stage. There were no mutually exclusive responsibilities, but we each gravitated to our individual sphere of expertise. I'll never forget our opening night at Enchanted Garden, the first club we opened in Queens. Steve went right to the bar and spent the whole evening hanging out with the kids. I went right to the DJ booth and spent the entire time playing with the lights and making sure the ambiance was just right. Together we were much more formidable than either of us would have been on our own. It was one plus one equals three.

Enchanted Garden did well and about two years later, in 1977, we opened Studio 54 in Manhattan. It was a tremendous hit. There were, of course, other nightclubs around at the time, but Studio 54 really took things up a notch. We had a theatrical approach and added a lot of glamour, design, and sophisticated special effects. We were like a couple of kids (I was thirty at the time) holding on to a lightning bolt that struck at the right place at the right time. Such great success at an early age was intoxicating, and as a result, Steve and I sort of lost our way. We began thinking that the rules didn't apply to us and we didn't pay income taxes. It was very stupid behavior. We got caught and were punished. We lost everything and ended up going to federal prison for thirteen months. It was devastating, humiliating, and almost destroyed us. If my parents had been alive at the time, it certainly would have killed them.

Doing time in prison is absolutely terrible. You are robbed of all human dignity and discretion. You are told when to eat and when to shower. It's a depressing state. I could never get comfortable and didn't thrive in that environment. But something that really helped me through my stay was reading books on great men who had either come from nothing and prospered or suffered travails in their lives and overcame them. I also remember being encouraged by David Halberstam's book, *The Powers That Be*. He wrote about the prominent media empires of this country like *Time*, the *New York Times*, the *Washington Post*, and CBS. They all had difficult interludes that interrupted their progress—but it was during those recesses that they decided to take another course and eventually achieved major success.

It was during my time in jail that I figured out what my next career move would be: hotels. At that time Donald Trump was doing a hotel called the Grand Hyatt New York and Harry Helmsley was doing the Helmsley Palace. The media was making a big deal about the rivalry between the old guard and the new guard. That type of competitiveness was alluring and dragged me in. I thought, *Steve and I can do that!* In my mind, it was an adjunct to what we had been doing: The nightclub business centers around taking care of your guests. They are not supposed to sleep over, but opening a hotel was a logical progression as far as I was concerned.

When Steve and I got out of prison, we were in major debt. We owed more than $1 million in legal fees, as well as some $750,000 in various taxes, penalties, and interest. In an effort to start paying off our debts, we were forced to sell the Studio 54 building in exchange for a promissory note.

Having nothing made me even more ambitious, and I was determined to get back to where I had been before losing it all. Unfortunately, the hotel business is very capital intensive and we couldn't get anyone to invest with us. In people's minds, we were nightclub guys. We were untested. No one wanted to risk their money to see how we would do in another field. As for banks, some wouldn't even allow us to open checking accounts, let alone lend us money. It was very discouraging.

David Geffen, a friend and role model, said something to me at the time that was very simple yet profound: "You don't begin until you begin." What he meant was that if I ever wanted to achieve success again I had to start somewhere. I couldn't expect to immediately build a multimillion-dollar hotel business. I had to get out there, start with what I knew, wait for opportunities to come my way, and respond to them. That's the secret: Don't allow yourself to get dispirited and give up.

One day the opportunity we had been waiting for presented itself. The person we had sold Studio 54 to couldn't pay us back, so we traded the promissory note in for his hotel on Thirty-eighth Street and Madison Avenue.

Like we did in the nightclub world, we wanted to create something outside the box and give our patrons an elevated experience. Utilizing a lot of the elements that made us so successful in the nightclub field—the stagecraft, the alchemy, the style—we put a lot of effort into renovating the hotel and reopened it as Morgans in 1984. It was another natural success. Our concept triggered the "boutique hotel" revolution and changed the entire industry. Following this, Steve and I bought another hotel, the Royalton, where we launched the concept of "lobby socializing," where the hotel lobby became a new kind of gathering place for guests and the city's residents alike.

But in 1989 our comeback together was cut short. Steve was hospitalized due to extreme dehydration, and two days later, at age forty-five, he was dead. I was traumatized. Steve and I had seen each other every day since 1964. I don't know who was the husband and who was the wife, but I loved him. The transition from working with Steve to branching out on my own was extremely difficult. I was anxious and insecure about whether I would be able to do it alone, but I realized I had no choice and picked up the baton where we left off. I've expanded a lot since then. I think Steve would be proud.

My whole tax evasion debacle—getting in trouble, going through the legal process, fighting it, going to jail, coming out, and getting on my feet again—cost me about ten years. That's the amount of time it took to get back to where I left off, both financially and emotionally. Thank God it all happened at an early age, and I didn't lose my enthusiasm or zest for life. Steve and I were able to pick ourselves up, dust ourselves off, and start over. I don't recommend prison to anyone, but I am certainly living proof that the system works. What I went through taught me the importance of playing by the rules and not cutting corners. I've always tried to take the high road since then. To that extent, it benefited me and made me stronger than I was before.

It took about thirty years before I was comfortable even speaking about the whole experience (being embarrassed about it in front of my kids was a huge factor). Although the wound has never fully healed, I am now happy to tell my story. I want to give back and help others who are trying to make good.

## IAN'S PEARLS

■ How one deals with obstacles is what separates the men from the boys. No matter what field you are in, there will always be stumbling blocks. Don't think about everything that can possibly go wrong. Just put one foot ahead of the other and, step-by-step, get everything done. I give the same advice to my daughter when she is overwhelmed with homework. I tell her to do one thing at a time and it will all get done. There is no other way.

■ Don't be afraid to follow your dreams, don't be afraid of trying something new, and don't be afraid of failure. Fear of failure often paralyzes people and prevents them from succeeding. They think: *If the decision I am making now is a mistake, it's all over.* That's not generally the case. There are very few things in life that you can't recover from. When you realize this, it's easier to make choices and keep moving forward. If you play it too safe, you won't get anywhere.

■ People naturally gravitate to their comfort zones. I built what I did around my sphere of capabilities. Stick to what you do well and don't do what you don't do well.

■ Sometimes your greatest assets can also be liabilities. To be successful in a creative field you need to have a visceral, emotional connection to what you are doing. Unfortunately, that enthusiasm and passion can't always be directed to where it serves you well. I, for example, believe that success is all about the details and I am a painstaking perfectionist. When this perfectionism makes its way into my personal life, it can be oppressive to others and myself. My wife and I recently put a lot of effort into our dream home. I think it came out picture-perfect. The problem is, I didn't want anybody to sit on any of the couches. That's the type of quality I wish I didn't have, but it helps to be aware of this and try to keep that kind of emotion where it belongs.

■ Walt Disney and Steve Jobs really inspire me because they pursued their visions and accomplished feats that others couldn't even imagine were possible. When Disney did his animation in the 1920s, the same techniques were available to everybody else—he just did it in a magical way. Same with Jobs. Other people were producing technologically advanced computer devices when he was, but the way he put his products together had a certain spark. You don't have to completely reinvent the wheel to be successful—the key is to do whatever you do in an imaginative, original way.

# GRAYDON CARTER
# VANITY FAIR EDITOR

**I GREW UP IN THE SUBURBS OF OTTAWA, A MODEL OF POST-EDWARDIAN PROTESTANT PROBITY AND THE CAPITAL OF CANADA. I WAS INTERESTED IN BECOMING A** playwright or an editor, but I had no role models. Ottawa was a government town and most of the adults I came into contact with were either diplomats or civil servants. My parents were warm and loving, but they provided little in the way of career guidance. Their complete inattention to me and my brother and sister might have proved a blessing.

I've come to realize that having all the space and freedom they afforded me was actually a huge gift. A lot of kids today are overloaded with after-school and weekend lessons—piano or Mandarin Chinese, things like that. I do believe that one of the most important things you can do for your children is to not overschedule them. Children need time to be bored and daydream; it's an important part of life. My daydreams motivated me and shaped my future.

Since I knew I'd eventually wind up with a white-collar job, I had a strong desire to taste life first—so I took on a number of blue-collar jobs when I was younger. In high school I worked for two weeks as a grave digger. When the weather turned cold in Canada, the ground would harden and so our local cemetery stockpiled the incoming beginning in October. When things began to thaw in the spring, they took on high school kids to help dig graves. I also sorted mail at the post office during Christmas breaks. One summer I worked in a bank and the next I stocked shelves in a big department store. For most of my high school summers I worked as a camp counselor and in the winters I was a ski instructor. I took a year off during college and worked for much of it as a lineman out in the Western Canadian prairies for the Canadian National Railroad. That was one of the most formative experiences of my

life. I lived with twenty other men in a box car that had been outfitted as a bunkhouse. Most of the others had criminal records for minor nonviolent crimes such as grand theft auto. They were a colorful crew. I got along with all of them, though. I was a good listener and learned to take my time fitting in. I made strong friendships, and by the time I came home, I realized that I could talk to just about anybody about anything. I read constantly and loved being out in the wild surrounded by rough men with difficult pasts. I went into the job with a great fear of heights, and by the end, like the others, I could climb a forty-foot telegraph pole without a safety belt. The workday was long and brutally hard, but I don't think I've ever loved a job so much. Also, I came back really fit.

I attended the University of Ottawa and Carleton University, but was eventually thrown out of both, due mainly to a general lack of attendance.

During my first year at the University of Ottawa, I ran into a clever, energetic fellow named Graham Pomeroy who taught me a great deal about turning an idea into a reality. He was starting a literary magazine called the *Canadian Review* and I signed on as his junior partner. My visions of the outside world were largely defined by magazines—*Time*, *Life*, *Esquire*, *Harper's*, the *New Yorker*, and the like. I loved magazines back then—and I still do. So I had the passion to jump into a new start-up but had absolutely no idea what to do. This was the early 1970s, before the Internet, fax machines, and computers. Many magazines were still set in hot type back then. I learned as I went along and grew to love every aspect of it all. At first, the publication was scholarly and, truthfully, not much fun to read—but we slowly built it into a sophomore version of *Harper's*, a magazine I admired. After a couple of years, Graham left and I became the sole editor. I poured everything I had into that magazine, working twelve to fifteen hours a day every day. I never took vacations and never went to class. I didn't have the time. I knew in the back of my mind that working on the magazine was going to prove to be the most worthwhile use of my time.

Some of my professors wrote for the *Canadian Review*. They were certainly not happy about my habit of skipping class, but they let me hang in there for a couple of years. At a certain point, the point at which I had too many incompletes to ever graduate, the school basically said, "You cannot graduate from here so there is no point in staying." I moved across town to Carleton University, where pretty much the same thing happened. The magazine took up most of my time, I never went to class, and after about a year and a half, I was asked to leave there as well.

Despite the fact that the *Canadian Review* had become quite popular, it did nothing but lose money. After giving it my all for five years, I sold our subscription list and assets to *Saturday Night* magazine, a competitor and a far superior publication. There is nothing worse than a long-term business failure. You pretty much know what's going to happen long before it goes under, and that whole period (about a year and a half in my case) was wretchedly painful. But, at the same time, I did it in concert with two wonderfully funny and supportive colleagues, Kate White and John Watts, and I now look back on the entire experience, even the darker moments, with great fondness.

My *Canadian Review* failure taught me an important but simple lesson: To succeed, your business has to have a point. I don't care what kind of a business it is; it has to provide something that others don't, and it has to do it well. The *Canadian Review* didn't have a point. It existed in large part because I wanted to have a magazine, and to the people who were our purported market that wasn't enough. Publications that are only there because the person behind them wants them to be rarely do well. Of course, some things that *have* a point fail too, but I have tried to make sure that everything I've done since then has a purpose.

After the *Canadian Review* shut down, I came to New York. I was encumbered by my student loan, but I had enough cash to enroll in an editing and publishing program at Sarah Lawrence College. When that ended, I returned home to Canada with the intention of moving to New York. I didn't have much money, just about $500 in cash and a credit card, but I figured that was probably enough to squeak out a month there looking for work. I wrote to everyone I had met through the Sarah Lawrence program (mainly magazine editors) and got appointments with most of them. I had never written a proper magazine article per se, but just as my money was running out, I was hired as a writer in the business section of *Time*. The Prince George Hotel on East Twenty-eighth Street had a special student rate of twenty-two dollars a night, so I moved there. I would leave in the morning dressed like a student then change into a suit when I got to the office. I'd change back into my student clothes before returning to the hotel. The twenty-two dollars was due every day. In cash.

Although I made some wonderful friends at *Time*, I had serious difficulties there and was in no way what you would call star material. In part, this was due to my own sweeping inadequacies. But it was also about the talent I was competing with. It was humbling to be surrounded by the extraordinary stable of young writers then working at the magazine: Michiko Kakutani, Frank Rich, Kurt Andersen, Walter Isaacson, Evan Thomas, Maureen Dowd, Alessandra Stanley, Jim Kelly, Steve Smith, Tom Sancton, and James Atlas. The list is long. All of them have gone on to have very distinguished careers.

At one point, Marshall Loeb, *Time*'s business editor, called me into his office and said, "Look, everyone really likes you, and you're a wonderful person, but you'll never make it in the magazine business. Maybe you should think about going into ad sales?" That was a low point. Still, I kept at it, working on my writing. (Fear of failure has always been a big motivating factor. I only got my American citizenship in 1999, so for most of my career, losing my job also meant the potential loss of my H-1B work visa, which would mean returning to Canada a failure.) My writing got better, but in the end I wasn't *Time* material, and after five years I left.

It was while I was at *Time* that my colleague and friend Kurt Andersen and I began talking about starting our own magazine: a satirical monthly about New York. By the time we began making more formal plans, I had moved to *Life* magazine, a few floors away in the Time & Life Building. I had the title, *Spy*, and over many lunches, we formulated a rough idea of what the magazine would be about. We teamed up with a young banker from Goldman Sachs named Tom Phillips, raised money, and took office space in the Puck Building on Lafayette Street. *Spy* proved to be successful and highly influential. If there is more fun to be had in the magazine business, I would be surprised. A stand-alone magazine in a conglomerate age is a tough place to be, though. And we were constantly short of money. At one point it just ran out, and we sold the magazine after five years to the adman Charles Saatchi and the investor Jean Pigozzi.

At that point I began thinking about starting up a biweekly New York newspaper and went on a listening tour to figure out how to accomplish this. I bumped into a man named Arthur Carter who owned the *New York Observer*, which was, at that time, a sleepy backwater broadsheet printed on salmon-colored paper. It had little in the way of audience or influence. Arthur hired me to redo the paper. I formulated six-month, twelve-month, and eighteen-month plans and set to work. Within three or four months, people were beginning to read it. At the ten-month mark, it had reached some sort of critical mass and a lot of people I knew seemed to be reading it. I began sending complimentary copies to about one hundred people every week, including a number of overseas Condé Nast editors I knew. Si Newhouse, whose family owns Condé Nast, took a trip to Europe twice a year to visit many of his international properties. Everywhere he went he spotted a copy of the *New York Observer* on somebody's desk. Not realizing that they were getting it for free (and probably not even reading it), he came back and asked if I'd like to meet with him. In 1992 Si hired me to be the editor of *Vanity Fair*, and I've been there ever since.

The first two years were, to put it mildly, rocky. Most of the advertisers and the staff looked on me with suspicion, and how could they not, given what we had written about many of them at *Spy*. The atmosphere was so poisonous that I didn't like to bring my kids into the office. But I'm a decent person, and since I treated the staff with respect, it gradually got better, and then it got truly wonderful.

Si has been like a father to me. A true role model. He has a Socratic method of sorting through problems that has been invaluable. And his wisdom covers you like a blanket. There is no finer man to work for. And after owning two magazines, it's a relief to have the financial aspects of a magazine in somebody else's hands. It frees you up to do what editors do best: edit.

## GRAYDON'S PEARLS

■  Nobody knows what they're doing at first. You have to find something you are interested in, throw yourself at it, do the best you can, and pick things up as you go along. I never saw myself as having a career path. I've sort of muddled through from one thing to the next and, for most people, that's just the way careers evolve.

■  You learn a lot more from mistakes than you do from successes. I tell my kids, "It's almost certain that you are going to make mistakes along the way. Try to make small ones, if you can, and think of them as opportunities to learn."

■  Even though I never ended up graduating from college, I think it's important for young people to try to do so. It was less difficult to get by without a completed education back when I was in my twenties. Rent was cheaper then and it was easier to live.

# KATHY IRELAND
## MODEL/ ENTREPRENEUR/ DESIGNER

**WHEN WE WERE KIDS, MY PARENTS ALWAYS ENCOURAGED ME AND MY TWO SISTERS TO WORK. IF WE WANTED SOMETHING, THEY'D SAY, "YOU'VE GOT TWO ARMS AND TWO** legs, go earn some money." They explained that if we looked around we could always find a way to do it. It was the 1970s and opportunities for women weren't as abundant as they are today, but my parents didn't see barriers or limits for us, so neither did we.

I was only four years old when my older sister and I started painting small rocks and selling them door-to-door. Three years later, I was washing neighbors' cars, watering their plants, and designing handbags to sell at the beach near our home in Santa Barbara, California. When I was eleven, my father showed me an ad in a local newspaper that read: "Newspaper carrier wanted, are you the boy for the job?" He knew exactly what kind of a reaction that would evoke from me. I immediately wrote to the paper saying that I was the *girl* for the job, and I got it.

Before my first day of work, my dad instructed me to give it 110 percent. He explained, "Customers expect the paper on the driveway, so you should put it on their front porch." I was excited to finally have some real responsibility and make some serious money. In the midst of my route, as I was biking from house to house, I saw a customer standing at the edge of his driveway. As I approached to hand him his paper, he yelled, "What are you doing here? You have no business doing this! It's a boy's job and you'll never last!" I didn't let him see me cry.

Only much later did I realize what a gift that incident was. The bag full of newspapers was a lot heavier than I had expected, and there were many days when I was exhausted and felt like quitting. But I didn't quit because I didn't want to give that man the satisfaction of being able to define me. Instead, I went on to win Carrier of the Year for my district three years in a row.

In my teenage years I developed into quite a tomboy, complete with a nasty habit of burping at people. When I was sixteen, my parents, thinking that a little finishing might be nice, enrolled me in a local modeling school. College wasn't within my family's means and my grades were definitely not good enough to get a scholarship, so when a scout from Elite Model Management visited the school and offered to represent me, I agreed. I figured that if I could get work as a model it would allow me to save some money to go to college or start a business some day.

Back then, agencies would send models on "go-sees" to get jobs. The people in charge of hiring would look us up and down and dissect us right in front of our faces. I was rejected a lot. It hurt at first, but I soon learned that it was just part of the process. Eventually, I started to book jobs. Within four years, I was featured in the *Sports Illustrated* swimsuit issue and went on to appear on the cover of that magazine three times.

Ironically, at only twenty-seven years old, I was already starting to feel like an aging model and wanted to start a business that was not dependent on my looks. I wanted to start my own brand and, with my background in fashion, felt an entrepreneurial career involving design might be possible. Recognizing that I wouldn't be able to do it on my own, I decided to hire Sterling/Winters, a management company, to help me get my vision off the ground.

For years we invested a lot of time, energy, and resources in various start-up ventures including a microbrewery, a skin-care line, and various art projects—but all of them failed. In 1993, when I was thirty years old and pregnant with my first child, I got an offer from a man named John Moretz to model a line of socks. It wasn't a very glamorous gig but rather than have a negative attitude and shoot him down I decided to make a counterproposal. What if we went into business together manufacturing and selling Kathy Ireland socks?

People laughed and said, "You can't start a brand with a pair of socks. That's never been done." But I reasoned that if I could be successful with a product that had no popular connection to me (unlike, say, swimsuits) it would mean that I was onto something. Besides, just because something hasn't been done before doesn't mean it can't work.

Before I made anything official, my team at Sterling/Winters, my family, and I tested the socks to ensure that we truly loved them. We also got to know John and the other people with whom he worked. We even did a surprise inspection at the sock factory to make sure we were comfortable with the working conditions there. Anybody can clean up when they know you're coming, but you learn a lot when you show up unexpectedly!

I took out a $50,000 personal loan to launch my own company, kathy ireland Worldwide, and a young Sterling/Winters executive and I loaded up our backpacks and went around the country presenting the socks to retailers. Doors were slammed in our faces. Some people didn't think the socks were good enough; others said that they loved the socks, but wondered if they could find something comparable but less expensive somewhere else.

Luckily, I was used to rejection from modeling, so I persevered. We were on a very tight budget and did whatever it took, including sleeping in airports, to save money. We viewed giving up material things as an investment, not a sacrifice.

Finally, a handful of sporting-goods stores decided to carry us. Then Kmart picked us up and soon asked for exclusivity. We were thrilled and signed with them. Our contract guaranteed a lot of security for many, many years and we soon expanded to include a complete line of apparel and accessories. As our brand grew, so did our spending. Gone were the days of airport sleepovers. We now had thirty-seven people on our payroll and bigger, fancier offices than we needed. Our financial advisors, however, assured us that our spending was far below the norm for a company of our size.

One day we got a phone call informing us that Kmart was having financial challenges. The next thing we knew, they were filing for bankruptcy. It was the largest bankruptcy in retail history—and a *total* shock. An avalanche of reality ensued. Guaranteed payments from Kmart stopped coming and my team members and financial advisors completely freaked out. Our bankers asked to meet with us immediately to discuss the situation. They explained that we were personally responsible for all the money we had borrowed from them and that if they didn't get paid back they'd be able to take away all of our homes. Things became very grim very quickly, to say the least.

Before Kmart's bankruptcy, we had started planning our brand's expansion into products for the home. Now we had to think on our feet and devise a new strategy that would somehow allow us to keep our heads above water. We sublet part of our office space and decided to focus all our energy on selling our existing products through various independent retailers. We scurried and scrambled, working around the clock.

Fortunately, Kmart was eventually able to get back on its feet under new management. At that point we moved forward with our plans to expand into the home area—but this time we would sell our products at both Kmart *and* independent retailers. Dealing with multiple stores is a lot of work, but it's enabled us to build a more solid foundation. No matter how good things look, they can always change. Whether it's a recession, a health crisis, a natural disaster, or something else, things frequently hit out of the blue and you need to be prepared. Don't put all your eggs in one basket—and *always* accomplish this in an ethical way. Also, never get too comfortable and be conservative with your spending.

When it comes to my business, I've always been ambitious and a control freak. Whether it's human resources, sales, marketing, design, quality control, or shipping, I involve myself in every aspect. I've also been inspired to embark on other projects, such as making a series of exercise videos and writing several books. I didn't realize what a toll it was taking on me. But then, in 2009, around the time that I was about to launch my book *Real Solutions for Busy Moms: Your Guide to Success and Sanity*, my son, Erik, got a camera and took a picture of me. When Chloe, my youngest of three children, saw it, she said, "Mom, you look pregnant!" The image took my breath away. Not only did I look overweight but I also looked overwhelmed, overstressed, and over everything!

There was a temptation to just delete the photo, but when I thought about the "real solutions" I was advising others to consider, running from the truth felt hypocritical. The photo of me on the book's cover was beautifully retouched; Erik's photo was *real*. I thought, *Let's just get the truth out there and learn from it.*

There's so much pressure on women to handle everything. Many of them, especially during their child-rearing years, tend to take care of everybody but themselves. At the time Erik photographed me, I was burning the candle at both ends and wasn't being healthy. Seeing the photo was a real wake-up call. While I'm still on top of all aspects of my expanding business, I've also learned the importance of delegating and that sometimes it's necessary to say no to good things in an effort to achieve great things.

I was at a conference where Barbara Walters, whom I greatly respect, said she didn't believe women could have it all. I disagree. We can have it all, but not all at the same time. Our lives come in seasons, and we have to prioritize our time in each. Besides, having it all looks different for each person because we all want different things.

Today, kathy ireland Worldwide designs and markets more than fifteen thousand products. We are in more than fifty thousand stores and in more than eighty countries. Our products and services include apparel, jewelry, housewares, home furnishings, flooring, lighting, replacement windows, publishing, entertainment, and all things bridal. I even bought Sterling/Winters in 2000.

For years we were able to operate kathy ireland Worldwide under the radar. As a private person owning a private company, that suited me just fine—but everything changed in 2012 when *Forbes* wrote an article about us. The ensuing publicity forced me out of my shell. It also made me realize that by keeping quiet I was being selfish. There are people everywhere struggling to get businesses off the ground. I've received so much wisdom from others who have shared their stories of failure and success with me. I now find it fulfilling and a joy to do the same for others.

## KATHY'S PEARLS

■ For many years I was ashamed of the gaps in my formal education. I was intimidated by other people's intellect and frequently felt like I had no business joining a conversation. Eventually, I realized that I didn't need to feel that way. Although I am a huge proponent of formal education, a real-life education can be extremely powerful. I also realized that I could take matters into my own hands and learn from reading and doing research on the Internet. There are no limits to the ways you can educate yourself. The smartest people I know never stop learning.

■ I have been harshly criticized at various points in my career. Back in my modeling days, a photographer very publicly said that I had a voice that could "kill small animals." When I first started in business, a journalist wrote an article referring to me as a bimbo. In 2010 I hosted ABC's Academy Awards red carpet segment and, among other negative comments, the chief marketing officer of a large public company tweeted that I was on drugs, looked pregnant, and that whoever hired me should be shot.

Although criticism often hurts, it can also be a gift. Even when it comes in a really nasty package, you have to examine it. It may simply give you the resolve to prove your critic wrong (as it did with the man I encountered on my first day delivering newspapers), but sometimes you'll find an opportunity to learn. For example, my voice was too high and squeaky—it was something I had to work on to be taken more seriously. Also, I did look a little stiff and uncomfortable while hosting the red carpet event.

Other times I have discovered an opportunity to teach. I called the journalist who wrote that I was a bimbo, for example, and said, "I have great respect for your profession, but I need to understand why you used that adjective to describe me. I have children who will read this. Also, when you write something that is not truthful, it hurts my business and there are many jobs at stake." He was extremely apologetic and we have become great friends. I made a similar call to the tweeting chief marketing officer. He also apologized and felt embarrassed about his actions. I could have let the comments go, but I knew that if I didn't confront these people they would be more likely to subject others to this kind of thing down the line.

■ People frequently tell me about business ideas they started but then abandoned—often because they encountered rejection or someone in their lives didn't like the idea. I say, "You stopped because of that? If you never fail, it means you are not trying hard enough."

■ It's essential to surround yourself with the right people. When it comes to core values, such as integrity and tenacity, being on the same page is important, but don't be afraid of working with people who take an approach that is different from yours. Diversity allows you to complement and learn from each other. Building a great team has always been a priority for me. As a result, most of us have been together through thick and thin for almost twenty-six years. Without this long-term strategy, our business could never have grown into what it is today.

# NITIN NOHRIA
# HARVARD BUSINESS SCHOOL DEAN

**MY FATHER GREW UP IN A SMALL RURAL VILLAGE IN INDIA WITH NO ELECTRICITY AND A VERY MODEST SCHOOL. THERE ARE HUNDREDS OF THOUSANDS OF THESE VILLAGES** in India. If you travel around the countryside and drive through one, children will run up to the window of your car. If you do as little as give them a pencil, they are the happiest people in the world. As you pull away, you wonder if any of them will ever escape those conditions. My father was one of those kids. Not only was he one of the first people in his village to finish high school; he then went on to get a scholarship to study engineering in college. After college, he got a scholarship to study management abroad. At thirty, he returned to India and became the CEO of a small company. He later became the CEO of a large company and then the president of several business associations. I learned from my father that there was no reason not to be ambitious and imagine that your life could be better. But it was also daunting to grow up with a parent like that. I often wondered, *How can I live up to what he's been able to accomplish?*

The greatest lottery of life is where you're born. I feel so fortunate to have been born into a wonderful family that was able to give me every opportunity I could have dreamed of.

In India, from first grade onward, students didn't just get grades, they were also ranked in their class. I always stood first or second. That was my entire measure of success. The government designed our curriculum, and everyone learned from the same set of prescribed textbooks. I was a sincere, high-performing kid, but I had no independent curiosity. In seventh grade that changed. My English teacher approached me one day and said, "How would you like to read books by Nobel Prize winners in literature?" He gave me about ten books from his own library. I don't know exactly what this teacher saw in me, but he clearly felt I could read more than the government thought I could. So off I went and I devoured works such as *The Good Earth* by Pearl S. Buck, *The Winter of Our Discontent* by John Steinbeck, and *Demian* by Hermann Hesse. I suddenly realized that I had an ability to explore the world. I gained a new confidence and, ironically, became a worse student (on paper) as a result. I began challenging what the teachers said and I would refuse to do things that I didn't find particularly compelling. Instead of focusing on completing my assigned homework

and maintaining good grades, I would go home and read whatever I wanted. I had become self-motivated, but I no longer stood first in my classes.

Like most middle-class families in India, my parents wanted their kids to be engineers or doctors. Those fields provided financial security, and since there was no wealth to pass down (CEO compensation in my father's time was modest because it was controlled by the government), that was very important to all of us. The top engineering school in India was the Indian Institute of Technology (IIT). At the time I graduated from high school, they allowed you to enter after either eleventh or twelfth grade. Acceptance was based solely on a notoriously difficult nationwide entrance exam that literally hundreds of thousands of students wrote. I applied after eleventh grade, as many others did, thinking I would, of course, get in.

People did not wait for admission letters back then, as the postal system was unreliable. IIT would post a list at the examination centers and some other public venues of about two thousand names, arranged by rank. If you were on that list, you'd been admitted; if you weren't, you hadn't. Everyone would crowd around the list when it went up. If anybody found a friend's name, they would shout it out. It was extremely nerve-racking. I went to the list, read through it, and didn't see or hear my name. I remember scanning it twice and then thrice thinking that I must have missed it. When I finally realized that I hadn't been admitted, I was devastated. I thought I was a failure and that I would be one for the rest of my life.

I remember going home and telling my father that I didn't think I was good enough for IIT and that I should just forget about becoming an engineer. He said, "Nothing is decided. You are still in school. Just write the exam again next year." So I wrote it again after twelfth grade, but the fear of failure was still in my soul. I completed the math section in the morning, and my father came to meet me during my lunch break. I approached him with a sinking feeling and said, "I don't think I'm going to make it. I'm not sure it even makes sense for me to write the rest." My father said, "Look, you're already here and you've prepared. Just write the afternoon portion. What difference does it make?"

One of the proudest moments of my life was standing in front of the IIT list later that year and seeing my name at number 650. I've never been happier to be ranked in the middle of anything!

I joined IIT Bombay to pursue a degree in chemical engineering, but it didn't come naturally to me. I somehow managed to become a decent student, but I realized that there were people who could do calculations in their sleep that I, as hard as I studied, would never be able to do. In my final years I finally got the chance to sign up for electives. I took classes that had a different quality—history, economics, literature, philosophy of science— and found I could grasp them spontaneously and easily. Any effort I put in delivered yet more. Finally, others looked at me and had the same experience I did watching them do mathematical equations. That's when I knew that as soon as I finished my chemical engineering degree I should pursue something else.

Influenced by my father's career, I wanted to go to graduate school in the United States and study business, but the reality was that I could not afford to do so if I didn't get a scholarship. Someone told me that PhD programs offered scholarships and masters programs didn't. Never thinking for a second that I'd wind up being a professor, I applied to a number of PhD programs and ended up enrolling at the Massachusetts Institute of Technology (MIT) in Boston, where I was fortunate not just to have been admitted but to have also received a fellowship. (I didn't even apply to Harvard because I thought it would be too difficult for me to be admitted.)

Unfortunately, I didn't get into any of the MIT dorms so, using what little scholarship money I had, I rented an apartment in a not-so-great part of town. You could describe my building as a quasi-immigrant tenement. Every single person living there was from a foreign country—and our landlord was from hell. The heat was utterly erratic. The radiator either didn't work at all or would emit a deafening clanging noise. We protested and told our landlord, but he did nothing. I was getting woken up all night long and was petrified about my academic performance (my scholarship was contingent on my continuing to have very good standing). So in January I packed up a sleeping bag and a change of clothes and moved into the MIT library. Literally. It was open twenty-four hours a day and there were nice couches for me to sleep on. I was studying until two or three in the morning most days anyway, and I was only sleeping four or five hours—so I would just do it all there and then go to the gym to shower and shave. It sounds deeply trying, but it was so much more comfortable than living in my apartment! I lived like that for six weeks until I got lucky and managed to get into MIT student housing.

I started by studying finance, which I felt made sense given my engineering background. But, once again, despite my long hours at the library, there were many students far more skilled than I was in that field. I realized that while I could get by doing finance I was never going to be extraordinary at it. My advisor encouraged me to branch out and study the subjects I was most interested in. I signed up for classes in less technical fields, such as organizational behavior, leadership, sociology, and psychology, and found that they came naturally to me. But I still studied nonstop.

PhD programs, at their core, orient you toward becoming an academic. The better I got to know my professors, the more the lives they led became appealing to me. I went to see my advisor and told him that I was interested in becoming an academic but was conflicted because I wanted to do "real" work. He said, "Being an academic is real work. It's just a different kind of real work." It sounds like such a trivial thing to hear, but his words helped me become a professor.

I graduated from MIT with a PhD in management and was very fortunate to receive offers to teach at several fine business schools. One of my options was Harvard Business School (HBS) in their organizational behavior program. If you think that Harvard is well-known in the United States, its reputation only grows exponentially the farther you go from Boston. When I was growing up in India, HBS was a fantasy. I used to wonder, *What does it take to be a part of an institution like that?* It was like a sacred place that was just beyond my reach. When I talked to my parents about the various job offers that I was thinking through, they felt I needed a lobotomy for even considering anything other than Harvard.

So I joined the HBS faculty at the age of twenty-six. You hear stories at HBS of how students are terrified of being "cold-called" by faculty members. Well, I must confess that on the first day I was as petrified as any student. My goal was to survive class without embarrassing myself and my family. All HBS classes are taught using the case method, where students are presented with a real-life business dilemma and put in the role of decision maker. Unlike teaching via lecture, where you can stand up and deliver what you've planned, there is a lot of student-teacher interaction in the case method, and there is uncertainty as to where it will lead. I spent at least twenty hours preparing for my first ninety-minute class and had a hundred worries running through my mind. What if the students didn't react the way I expected them to? How would I handle it if a student didn't want to answer a question? If their answers go all over the map, how will I get them back on track? If a student says something foolish, how do I help him or her not feel ashamed?

Thankfully, that initial class turned out fine, but for the first several years, I still prepared obsessively and worked incredibly hard. Most mornings I would arrive at my office by five a.m. and fourteen-hour days were par for the course. (It now takes me about ninety minutes to prepare for a ninety-minute class, but I still get a twinge of anxiety whenever I go in front of any classroom!)

During my first year at HBS, I wondered if sometimes I wasn't being taken seriously because I am Indian and didn't fit what people expected a business school professor to look like. I had a mentor named Bob Eccles who was the head of my unit. We used to write cases together and would go to different companies to interview people about specific situations. In these conversations, I noticed that everything would be directed at Bob. Yes, he was the senior colleague, but I didn't think that was the reason. I couldn't tell whether it was discrimination or simply the awkwardness of another person not knowing how to pronounce my name—but it was definitely happening. One day I just decided to be assertive and inject myself into the conversations. I discovered that if I was proactive in participating and shaping the discussion people would talk to me. From that experience I learned that I could influence how people interacted with me.

My time in the United States has been a continual living of the American Dream, and I feel grateful for the many opportunities I've been given. However, if it wasn't for my English teacher in seventh grade, I don't think I would have ever had the confidence to believe I had anything useful to offer. Instead, I was inspired to explore and develop my own point of view. This has been a big part of what's allowed me to flourish at HBS and realize things I never would've imagined possible. I went from being a professor to a unit head to senior associate dean. Then in 2010 I got a magical phone call from Drew Gilpin Faust (president of Harvard University) informing me that she would like me to be the dean of Harvard Business School. It was beyond any dream I could have imagined. Coincidentally, my father and mother, who visit me once a year from India, were with me that day. I can't tell you how fortunate I felt to be able to share that moment with them. Our family had sure come a long way from the rural village in India where my father grew up.

## NITIN'S PEARLS

■ Understanding your strengths and weaknesses can take a long time and can even be a painful process, but it's one of the most important things to do in life. I feel fortunate to have found a career that I am passionate about and am thankful that I allowed myself to switch course and dedicate myself to this new path. But the lesson to take away from my story is not to change paths the moment you discover something's difficult for you. If you give up at first blush, you'll never succeed at anything because nothing worth doing is easy. Give whatever you do your full effort, but at the same time keep your eyes open. If you discover, even by accident, what you're truly spectacular at and can pursue it, I recommend doing so.

■ Be generous and don't worry about keeping score. My grandfather didn't have a lot of money but he was amazingly generous. He and his circle of friends used to play an Indian card game in which a very small amount of money changed hands. I used to visit him every summer vacation and can't remember anyone my grandfather hadn't deliberately lost to before they left his home. No guest could leave without a meal, and everyone was always welcome to sleep over. People my grandfather had worked with or had recently met would regularly ask him for help, and he would always try to do whatever he could. We predicted that about a hundred family members and friends would attend my grandfather's funeral, but many more people came to pay their respects, including several people none of us even knew. My grandfather was loved and admired in life and death. He made a huge impact on a lot of people, including me. I try to teach my students to behave as he did. When you are generous, you will always feel good about yourself. If life ends up being generous in return, as it usually does with giving people, then you will have greater joy.

# MARINA ABRAMOVIĆ
## ARTIST

**I WAS BORN IN BELGRADE IN 1946 JUST AFTER THE SECOND WORLD WAR. MY PARENTS WERE BOTH PARTISANS AND NATIONAL HEROES. THEY WERE VERY HARD-CORE AND** were so busy with their careers that I lived with my grandmother until I was six. Until then, I hardly even knew who my parents were. They were just two strange people who would visit on Saturdays and bring presents. When I was six, my brother was born, and I was sent back to my parents. From that point on, my childhood was very unhappy. I grew up with incredible control, discipline, and violence at home. Everything was extreme. My mother never kissed me. When I asked why, she said, "Not to spoil you, of course." She had a bacteria phobia so she didn't allow me to play with other children out of fear that I might catch a disease. She even washed bananas with detergent. I spent most of my time alone in my room. There were many, many rules. Everything had to be in perfect order. If I slept messily in bed, my mother would wake me in the middle of the night and order me to sleep straight. (To this day, when I'm in a hotel, people think I didn't even sleep there because the bed always looks so neat.) Whenever my brother cried, it was blamed on me, and I was beaten. I was beaten regularly for other reasons too and I started getting severe bruises. When one of my baby teeth fell out and the bleeding wouldn't stop, everyone thought I might have hemophilia so I was put in the hospital for a year. That was the happiest, most wonderful time of my life. Everybody was taking care of me and nobody was punishing me. I never felt at home in my own home and I never feel at home anywhere.

Because of my constant isolation as a child, I started painting and drawing very early, at about three years old. This was one of the few things my mother supported and encouraged.

There was never any doubt in my mind that I wanted to be an artist. I am really lucky in that respect because I didn't have to spend time finding myself like a lot of others do. When I was twelve, I had my first art show. I remember being jealous of Mozart when I learned that he had his first concert at seven.

I attended the Academy of Fine Arts in Belgrade and later got a postgraduate degree at the Academy of Fine Arts in Zagreb. I began painting clouds and was constantly looking at the sky for inspiration. One day I was lying on the ground looking up and a few supersonic planes flew over me and made these incredible lines, like drawings. I watched them appear, form, then disappear; and then the sky was blue again. It was incredible. I immediately went to the military base and asked friends of my father's if they could give me twelve supersonic planes to make a drawing in the sky. They called my father and said, "Get your daughter out of here. She is completely nuts!" But after that, I never went to the studio again. It was almost like a spiritual experience, and I realized that I could make art from practically nothing. I could use water, fire, earth, wind, myself. It's the concept that matters. This was the beginning of performance for me.

At the time, performance was not considered a form of art. It didn't exist on its own as a medium in school and it was even seen as ridiculous. This was my hell! But I knew that I was on the right path and began performing wherever and whenever I could. I became part of a student cultural center in Belgrade, which was kind of an oasis for me. There were six of us there. I was the only woman and the only one doing performance. We put on art shows together—each doing our own thing—because it was stronger than trying to do it alone.

Eventually, I began getting invitations to perform on my own and I started pushing my physical and mental limits. In one performance, for example, I tried to explore the relationship between performer and audience. I placed seventy-two objects on a table that people were allowed to use on me in any way they chose. Among the items were a feather, a rose, honey, scissors, a scalpel, a whip, a gun, and a single bullet. For six hours I allowed the audience to manipulate my body and actions. I felt violated. They cut up my clothes and stuck rose thorns in my stomach. One person aimed the gun at my head, and another took it away. It was an aggressive atmosphere. I was criticized by my professors and often completely ridiculed by the press. But I kept doing what I was doing and hoped that my form of art would be accepted. I was very strong willed.

All this time, by the way, I remained living at home and was constantly being punished by my mother. It was scandal after scandal after scandal. She would burn art I made and didn't allow me to be out of the house past ten p.m. But it never even crossed my mind to leave. At the time there was really no other choice. Several generations in the same house was how people lived in Eastern Europe. It's kind of insane when you think about it. I had to do all my performances in the mornings and afternoons because I had to be home by ten p.m.!

On my twenty-ninth birthday I received an invitation to perform on a Dutch TV program. When I arrived at the airport in Amsterdam, I was met by another artist, a man named Ulay, who was to be my guide. We discovered that we had the same birthday and much more than that in common. We immediately fell terribly in love. I returned to Belgrade, but we got lovesick and planned to meet in Prague, which is between Amsterdam and Belgrade. We decided we would live together in Amsterdam and work together too. It was one of those magical moments where everything comes together. So at twenty-nine I ran away from home to live with Ulay. I literally escaped. My mother went to the police, told them that I was missing, and gave them a description of me. The police officer said, "But how old is she?" When he learned I was twenty-nine, he made my mother leave.

At first, I had trouble adjusting to my newfound freedom. While on one level I hated and rebelled against all my restrictions in Belgrade, both the political control and my home life, I also fed on them. In Amsterdam I felt the need to create my own restrictions and started building instructions for myself in my performances. To this day, every performance I do is based on discipline and specific instructions that have to be executed in front of the public. It's become the frame I make my work within.

All I wanted to do was be an artist. I didn't want to work in a restaurant or do any other job, so Ulay and I decided to live together in a van. It was the most radical but also the simplest decision I have ever made. It was really the only way we could exist. We had no money and the performances we did hardly paid. We lived like that for five years and it was bliss! We spent most of our time with the peasants in the countryside where we helped milk the goats and make pecorino cheese in exchange for food. Otherwise, we would stay by friends or just park anywhere. I knew every shower in every gasoline station. We would make phone calls to different places and ask if we could perform. We were always waiting for invitations to perform. Wherever we went, we would open the back of the car and ask people to come meet us. That was our lounge. We even had a car guest book that all our visitors would sign. We became a kind of ideal couple. People looked up to us because we didn't make any compromises.

We were once invited to perform at a festival at the museum in Bologna, Italy. Our performance was called *Imponderabilia*, and it actually ended up becoming pretty famous. We rebuilt the entrance of the museum so it was smaller, and we stood naked on either side of the door facing each other. If you wanted to enter, you had to turn sideways and face either Ulay or me to get through. Our reasoning was that if there were no artists there would be no museum, so we thought that the idea of two artists standing naked at the entrance would be very poetic. We arrived in Bologna completely broke and out of gas, but we were promised about a $250 fee. At the time that was huge for us (we could live on that amount of money for about three months). Every morning all the artists would ask to be paid. The Italians

were very nice and gave us food, but every day they had a different excuse as to why they could not pay us: Tomorrow is the strike, the day after the bank was closed, the uncle of the secretary forgot the key... I knew that if we finished the performance without getting paid, we never would be paid. On the last day, right before the museum was about to open (as the public was already lining up outside), Ulay decided to do something extreme. Already completely naked, he went up to the third-floor office, opened the door, and said, "Where is our money?" The woman working there was shocked. She screamed like hell, then took the key, opened the safe, and gave it to him. The money had, of course, always been there—they just didn't want to give it to us. So Ulay was standing there naked, holding $250 in lira, which was a lot of bills, and he didn't know what to do with them. We didn't trust anybody there so he looked into the rubbish, found a plastic bag, wrapped the money in it, and put it in the water tank of the museum's public toilet. It was the only place to hide it. And then we went to perform. The whole time, we were thinking, *Is the money going to be flushed?* In the end, we got the money and it was safe. We were the only artists paid for performing at that festival!

Ulay and I were very, very happy for nine years. We were a complete unit, professionally and emotionally, and we began to make a name for ourselves in our field. But then somehow the pressure of being the ideal couple and the pressure of our success were too much for him. To me, art was everything. To Ulay, it was not. We grew apart and he started to become unfaithful. It was very heavy and difficult for me to deal with. For three years I could not admit failure. I pretended to everyone that everything was still great. But it got to a point where I felt like if I did that any longer I would get cancer and die.

For eight years Ulay and I had been requesting permission to do a performance piece on the Great Wall of China. Our plan was to start at opposite ends, walk toward each other, and get married when we met. By the time the Chinese finally said yes, our relationship was over. I have never been one to give up a good opportunity, so we decided to still walk toward each other but say good-bye instead when we met. It was extremely painful. To make things worse, I knew at the time that Ulay had made his Chinese guide pregnant and would soon be having a child with her.

When things ended with Ulay, I was forty. I felt fat, ugly, and unwanted. I couldn't fall back on my work because it was nonexistent; everything I had been doing was with Ulay. With nowhere to go, I decided to make theater from my life and created a piece where I actually played myself on stage. I invited Ulay and his then wife—he married the Chinese guide—to be in the production. I said good-bye to Ulay and my old life. It was a crazy moment. I have had very little contact with Ulay since then, and our relationship has never really been settled, but playing my life out on stage was very therapeutic and it's something I still do.

When I was growing up, my private life was not valued. The noblest thing one could do in my family was to sacrifice everything for a cause. Art became my cause and it's still everything to me. I dedicate all the energy in my body to my work and have completely sacrificed a more conventional personal life for it. I have no partner and no children, but I'm very proud of myself for always doing what I want, no matter what the cost and no matter how long it's taken. I've turned into a soldier, actually. (I've turned into my parents!) I have hundreds of ideas every day. I wake up in the morning with this urge to create; it's almost like I am in a fever. Every single day is structured. I work, work, work, and my curiosity never ends. The only time I feel tired and old is if I look back on all I've done, because it's a lot. I'm also like a clinical case: If you don't get love from your family, you turn to other things to get it. I get the love I need from my audience. Without the public, my performances wouldn't exist because I am not motivated to perform alone. The public completes my work and has become the center of my world.

When a young artist comes to me and says, "I want to be famous and rich," I ask him to leave because this is not the reason to make art. Those things are just side effects that you may be lucky enough to achieve. Your reason for doing art should be much deeper. You know you are an artist if you have to do art—it's like breathing and you have no choice. Nothing should be able to stop you.

## MARINA'S PEARLS

■  The success of an artist is generally measured by how much he can sell his work for, especially in America. This is shocking to me. How can you measure people like that? There have been so many artists who were never recognized and didn't sell anything during their lifetime, but when they died, their work sold for millions. El Greco took a hundred years to be recognized as an artist and his work is sublime. If you don't sell anything, it doesn't mean that you are not a good artist. Okay, it could be that you produce bad art—but sometimes it's because your work is ahead of society. I think that a good work of art has many lives.

■  In postgraduate school I had a special professor who told me something I will never forget. He said, "If you draw with your right hand and become so skilled that you can even close your eyes and make any kind of drawing, immediately change to the left. Repetition will kill you." Often, once an artist has achieved a certain level of success and is accepted and recognized by the public, he stops growing. He is afraid to experiment and go in other directions because he could fail.

It is really important for an artist to accept failure and be true to himself. When you experiment, you never know how things will turn out. It could be great or it could be really

bad. I certainly don't like all the art I have created, and I have put on some terrible performances! During them, I remember thinking, *Oh, my God, this is such bullshit*, but I couldn't stop because there was an audience and I had obligations. When I was painting, I would sometimes work on one piece for a very long time and it would get worse and worse and worse. But then I would move on to a new painting and, in three minutes, I would be there. What you learn from one failure can be concentrated and transmitted to the next thing you do.

■ When artists reach a certain status, it's important for them to open themselves up, to be generous, and to help the younger generation of artists. I, for example, have been teaching for more than twenty-five years, and I have created an organization (which is no longer active) that helped young artists to find galleries and to show at international festivals. I am currently creating an institute for time-based immaterial arts called the Marina Abramović Institute. As part of this, I will also help the artists financially.

■ It's important to put the idea of dying in your daily life because it helps you to appreciate your existence on this planet. Death can come at any second and change everything. It can be the death of a loved one or your own. People spend endless time on total insanity, thinking that they will be here forever. Life is temporary. Make every day meaningful and don't spend time on bullshit.

# TOM SCOTT
# NANTUCKET NECTARS CO-FOUNDER

**WHEN I GRADUATED FROM BROWN, MY GOALS WEREN'T TOO LOFTY. I REMEMBER BEING INFLUENCED BY BARTENDERS. I WOULD LOOK AT THEM AND THINK,** *I want to live that life.* I wanted to live a *cool* life, and to me that meant being in a fun, relaxed environment and not having to wear a coat and tie.

So I moved to Nantucket, lived in my car, and got a job driving a taxi. My dad used to say that I was kind of a bum—and it was true. I worked a ten-hour shift and would always arrive a few minutes late and leave a few minutes early. That's just how I was. I barely did what was required, nothing more.

One day a friend asked if I wanted to try to sell muffins off a boat. The plan was to peddle to the other boats in the harbor. By this point, I had come to the conclusion that I eventually wanted to work for myself, and the idea sounded fun so I went for it.

When the Fourth of July rolled around, I planned to work instead of going out. My friends were incredulous. I realized that since graduating in mid-May I had worked every single day around the clock without complaint. I remember thinking, *Not being a bum is actually fun!* It reminded me of playing fort as a kid when my friends and I would pick a mission, devise a set of rules, decide who was going to be the captain and who was going to be the sergeant, and then organize everything to make it succeed. What we were doing was essentially creating imaginary jobs for ourselves. The grown-up version of the game—my floating store—didn't feel too different. The excitement was still mostly in the interaction with other people.

Over the next two years, six of my friends joined in, and we dramatically expanded the scope of the business. Our slogan was "Ain't nothing these boys won't do." One friend, Tom First, and I shared the same playful personality. One night he blended up a peach juice based on his memory of something he'd tasted in Spain. Within about seventeen seconds, we thought, *This is what we have to sell off the boat!* It happened that fast. We came up with the name Nantucket Nectars and spent the entire winter testing all sorts of fruity concoctions. We were obsessed.

During that first summer, we made our juices at home and sold them in a motley assortment of containers. We used everything from milk cartons and wine bottles to little wax-paper cups. We would keep hawking until we sold out, and then we would go home and make more. This was fine with everyone in the harbor, but when we finally approached stores, expectations were way different. The stores didn't want to see us every day. They wanted to order a certain quantity and sell it over a prolonged period of time. We'd deliver what they requested, but then it would go bad. We were, like, "Oh, yeah, *going bad*. What do we do about that?" We realized that we had to pasteurize, and once that entered the equation, we stepped into another realm.

Our quiet game of fort rapidly evolved into an all-out war. We were now in an arena with competitors, Snapple, for instance, that I had never even heard of. We wanted to win the battle of who tasted the best, but we also had to compete on price, size, distribution, promotion, and advertising. We were constantly running low on money and we soon realized that in order to stay afloat and grow we would have to raise some. We literally went to the library and researched "how to raise money." Since we had met some successful business people on Nantucket as customers, we started by pitching it to them. Later on, we went to the banks.

Nantucket Nectars was always on my mind. I worked seven days a week, usually until eleven p.m., for the first eight years. The only breaks I remember taking were to go out at night and blow off steam—but I never took days off. Not even Saturdays or Sundays. I never woke up and thought, *Oh, man, I've got to go to work today*. I didn't feel that way. I *chose* to go.

But the larger our business grew, the more room there was for things to go wrong. And it seemed like almost everything did. Trucks crashed, bottles blew up, juice spoiled, factories broke down, and we were sued. There was one day when all the money we had in the world was sitting in a vat of incorrectly formulated orange-mango juice. We had used way more peach than was called for, and it turned the juice into this black brew that tasted of alcohol. If we threw it away, we'd go broke. We had to figure out a way to salvage it. I think we ended up adding a bunch of apples and mixing the juice into some new flavor that we could bottle and sell.

The bottom line was that in terms of distribution, sales, marketing, and manufacturing, we had taken on way more than we could handle. Our ship began to leak in a bunch of tiny little places, and before we knew it, we were hemorrhaging about $250,000 a month. That's, uh, never good. I was super panicked. We had a line of credit with the Bank of Boston, which we needed in order to survive, and right around Christmas they pulled it. When the bank calls and says, "You can't borrow any more money," that's it. People wonder what it means to "go out of business." It usually means that you ran out of money. You literally can't turn the lights on back at the office the next day. We were right at that threshold. And then I got another call from our main individual investor who pretty much bawled me out. I remember crying. Nighttime was the worst. Anytime you're depressed, the night sucks.

But then a miracle happened. Fleet Bank swooped in and said, "We'll back you, but you have three months to turn a profit." It was part luck and part expectation that we had the potential of being a good story. With our young laid-back bohemian image, we had made a name for ourselves around Boston. If Nantucket Nectars did work out, Fleet could get mileage out of marketing us as one of their success stories—and that's what happened. They ran ads in *Newsweek* and *Time* about how they helped us grow our business. It ended up being great for both of us.

So we had to turn a profit by the end of March—even if it was only a dollar. The thing I remember most about that time is that the X's and O's of what needed to be done were clear, but what wasn't clear was how to execute them. The best part was that our employees were really dedicated and cared. One woman said, "I'm going to exercise every day until we turn a profit!" Another declared he would ride his bike to work every day until we did. (It was five miles, it was January, and it was cold.) I vowed not to shave. And we made it. We did it! I have no doubt that it's because of those little goofball stories. Before that, I thought being a successful business leader was all about smarts and the ability to have a perfect view of the future. But I came to realize that while you need a decent view of the future what's most important is being able to inspire your troops to be passionate, to believe what you believe, and to help you march in that direction.

My dad has been a huge influence on the way I go about things. He's a former marine and an athlete who became a lawyer and started his own firm. He always believed in the American Dream. Whenever something went wrong, he'd say things like "You gotta get out there and try again!" and "You gotta believe." That's what I was raised with, and it absolutely stuck with me.

I was twenty-five or so the first time I heard somebody refer to me as an "entrepreneur." I had no idea what that meant. That's how uncommon the term was in those days. Most Brown graduates went down the more traditional career paths. My friends were at places in their lives where they had company cars, suits, and memberships to country clubs. It was tough when I would go home to D.C. for holidays. I didn't have any nice clothes, and when I said I had started a juice company called Nantucket Nectars, no one had heard of us. I felt low, but at the same time this was a big motivator.

There was definitely a time when I thought that only supermen and superwomen achieved success. You know, people who had all this stuff that I didn't. But a few small pivotal events convinced me that successful people were really just normal people. The one I remember most was when Tom and I met with the CEO of Pepsi. To my surprise, there was a lot about the beverage industry that we knew and he didn't. We lived it on the streets day in and day out; he lived it in boardrooms day in and day out. It was two different sides of the same business. I remember thinking, *He's kinda like my dad.* You know, just a normal guy. I understood everything he said, and I told him things that I believed and he agreed with me. I remember leaving the meeting thinking, *Wow!*

I saw Tipper Gore speak right around that time, probably around 1993. She said, "My husband and the president are completely ordinary men in an extraordinary situation." That also stuck with me. I thought, *That's what's going on here. We are all totally ordinary people with a chance to create extraordinary situations for ourselves.* Being successful is a choice.

Jack Welch is a Nantucket guy, and I used to see him around the island. He also reminded me of my dad; they look alike, they talk alike, and they have a very similar tough style. I knew that Jack Welch ran General Electric, but in my mind that meant he had a few lightbulb factories. You know, big deal. But then I would hear people talk about him with such reverence. I was, like, "You mean that guy? *That guy?*" As time went on, I realized what a business legend he was, and for some reason, he would always pop into my brain as inspiration. I would think, *If I don't succeed, it's because I don't have the courage to make choices like Jack Welch.* You know that expression, "What would Jesus do?" For me it became "What would Jack Welch do?"

I once heard the quote, "Everyone's on the road to success, it's just that most people step off." That pretty much sums up how I see things. My decision with Nantucket Nectars was to not step off. I ended up creating an extraordinary situation for my regular self by staying on the road. I absolutely believe that.

## TOM'S PEARLS

■ When we first started the business, if the number 1 represented how hard I thought it would be, it ended up being more like the number 1,000. It was that much harder. But I think being naïve helped. Because I didn't know what was coming around the corner, I didn't live around the corner. I lived in whatever was right in front of me at that moment. If you start off focusing on everything you'll eventually have to figure out, and all the problems you'll eventually have to solve, it can be overwhelming, even debilitating. You don't need to know all the answers right away. Everything has an organic time and place. Being patient can be a huge advantage.

■ When someone graduates from school and they ask, "What's a smart business to get rich off of?"—I get nervous for them. You have to be passionate about what you do because when the forty million problems start you'll need that energy to keep you going. If I didn't love what I was doing, there's no way I would have made it through the trying times.

■ Most business endeavors require some degree of teamwork. If you are going to partner up with someone, you should spend a great deal of time and energy getting to know their character. Intelligence and drive are important, but fairness, loyalty, and all around good morals are essential. Without those qualities, everything else is useless. I have not always gotten it right, but I feel incredibly fortunate to have established my partnership with Tom First. We used to tell each other, "I'll focus on your money and you focus on mine," because we knew that we would always look out for and support each other. The level of trust we built made both of us infinitely more capable.

# WENDY KOPP
# TEACH FOR AMERICA FOUNDER

**THE SUMMER AFTER MY FRESHMAN YEAR AT PRINCETON UNIVERSITY I GOT A JOB WORKING FOR THE FOUNDATION FOR STUDENT COMMUNICATION, A STUDENT-RUN** organization designed to bring students and business leaders together to discuss pressing social issues. My job was to go out with a partner and ask corporate executives to sponsor our conferences and advertise in a little magazine we put out.

Our very first meeting was with the CEO of a company in St. Louis. We went to his office and gave him our presentation. When we were done, he swiveled around in his chair, pointed out his window, and said, "See that neighborhood down there?" He proceeded to go into a description of the unfortunate circumstances of the kids growing up in St. Louis's inner city then asked, "Why would I ever support your organization when there are so many more pressing needs?" I was stunned. I thought, *I can't continue with this job. I can't ask another person to give money to this organization because that man is totally right.* I ultimately decided to follow through on my summer commitment because I didn't want to leave the organization in the lurch, but that CEO's words never left me. I knew from then on that I wanted to find a way to address the most important needs.

Throughout my years at school, I was a very driven, involved, and overachieving student—the kind of person who always thought things through and had a plan. But when my senior year rolled around, I realized that, aside from my desire to make a difference in the world, I had no idea what I wanted to do after graduation. Lost and frustrated, I descended into a major funk and was unable to move ahead with anything—for months. The issue of my future weighed on me all my waking hours.

It was 1989 and I was a member of what people were calling the Me Generation. All we supposedly cared about was making money and leading luxurious lives. Investment banks, management-consulting firms, and brand-management firms were coming to campus recruiting seniors to sign up for their two-year corporate training programs. Those were the only kinds of opportunities banging on our doors and it seemed like just about everyone was applying. I halfheartedly applied to one firm in each sector.

As I continued to soul-search about my future, I found myself simultaneously becoming increasingly engrossed in another issue: the inequity in educational outcomes based on the circumstances of birth. Growing up, I attended public schools in a homogenous upper-middle-class community in Dallas. The expectation was that everyone would go to college. And there was money to spare: $100,000 scoreboard hung above our $3 million football stadium. Because of the high quality of my schools and the support provided by my family, I graduated with a very solid education and was able to do well in college without locking myself into solitary confinement at the library.

While Princeton University might not seem like the most likely place to become concerned about what's wrong in education, it was there that I first got to know students who had attended public schools in lower-income areas. They were smart, driven people, but they initially struggled to meet the university's academic demands. I realized that although our country aspires to be a place of equal opportunity, where you're born really determines your educational prospects. During my senior year, I helped organize a conference to discuss this issue through the Foundation for Student Communication. It was during that conference that everything came together. I thought, *Why aren't we being recruited as aggressively to commit two years to teach in low-income communities as we are to work on Wall Street?* I decided that America should have a national teacher corps of top recent college graduates who would do just that. I knew that I wasn't the only person in my generation searching for something meaningful to do with my life. I was sure that many of my peers would jump at this kind of chance.

As a senior at Princeton, I was required to write a thesis but, thanks to my funk, I had been unable to decide on a subject. I now had my answer: I would write about my teacher corps idea. I must have been the last person in my department to declare a topic, and as a result, I was striking out right and left finding anyone to be my advisor. Someone pointed me in the direction of Professor Marvin Bressler, the chair of the sociology department, who was a big advocate of mandatory national service. He met with me, read my proposal, and said, "This is not an academic thesis. It's more of a national advertising campaign for teachers—but if you recommend mandatory national service, I'll be your advisor." I accepted the condition with absolutely no intention of following through, and I was off.

I became increasingly excited about my idea—about both the immediate impact that talented recent graduates could have on students and the long-term importance of shaping the priorities of the graduates themselves, who would ultimately shape our nation's consciousness, policies, and practices. At the same time, my job search wasn't going so well. It didn't yield a single offer! I remember standing at a pay phone hearing the Morgan Stanley recruiter—my last remaining corporate possibility—tell me that I was not the right fit for the firm. The moment I hung up I made my decision; I would start the teacher corps. If I wasn't going to do it, then who was?

My thesis quickly morphed into an extremely ambitious plan for creating this corps. I wrote that we would inspire thousands of people to apply the first year through a grassroots recruitment campaign led by student leaders, select five hundred of them, enlist the help of experienced teachers and teacher educators to train them, and convince school districts to hire them as teachers in communities across the country. I developed a budget showing this would cost $2.5 million in the first year.

Fearing what Professor Bressler might say if he knew what I was actually writing, I avoided seeing him until I turned my thesis in. I was called into his office two days later. I was worried when I entered the room, but it turned out he liked it! He said, "Do you know how hard it is to raise $2,500 let alone $2.5 million?" That was his big focus. I told him that although I didn't know or have any connection to Ross Perot, I was positive he would help. Having grown up in Dallas when Mr. Perot led a campaign to improve Texas schools, I was certain he would love my idea. Professor Bressler set me up with the head of development at Princeton to explain the challenges in store for me. But their concerns went in one ear and out the other. Blessed with the advantage of naïveté and inexperience, I didn't know enough to realize how lofty my vision was, and I went forth in an effort to raise seed money. Without a grant, I would have to get a real job to support myself upon graduation and there would be no teacher corps.

I began by sending my thesis to Mr. Perot and thirty other corporate executives (some of whom I targeted because they were quoted in an article *Fortune* magazine had done about corporate America stating they needed to commit themselves to education reform). Others were randomly selected. Amazingly enough, some of those letters landed in the right hands and I got a few responses and meetings. So, while my classmates spent April and May unwinding from our thesis ordeal and celebrating our imminent graduation, I dressed up in a suit and took the six-thirty a.m. train into Manhattan for one appointment after another. It was completely worth it. Although I never heard back from Mr. Perot, Mobil Oil Corporation (now ExxonMobil) ended up making a seed grant of $26,000 and Union Carbide said I could work out of their offices in Manhattan.

Many people think that success is about coming up with a big idea, inventing something new, or finding the perfect job. Those are definitely great starting points, but I believe that success is really dependent on how you handle everything that happens thereafter. I named my venture Teach For America and spent the whole summer after graduation trying to

build support for it while living off of the seed grant. (The original name was simply Teach America, but I added the "For" when I found out that another company had already laid claim to that title.) I reached out to hundreds of people—among them educators, funding sources, business leaders, and wealthy individuals. Gaining access was the hardest part. For every one hundred letters I wrote (there was no e-mail at the time), I would get just a couple of meetings. Some folks thought my idea was good, and others didn't. Some thought it ran counter to what needed to be done to improve teaching. They felt that teachers needed to be trained in campus-based graduate programs as doctors and lawyers were. Others thought I was too young and inexperienced to lead this effort. Almost everyone advised me to start smaller (with, say, fifty teachers instead of five hundred). It was very stressful because I believed strongly that my vision had to happen, and it's very hard when others don't share your views.

I remember a particularly disconcerting meeting with a highly regarded school super-intendent. He was incensed by the notion that privileged recent college graduates could actually make an impact on the hardest-to-staff schools and was very vocal about it. He told me I was wasting his time and that he didn't need more do-gooders teaching in his district. I found myself exhausted and crying in my rental car afterward. I had a similar encounter with a longtime advocate for children in low-income communities. He tried his best to counsel me out of my enterprise because he was concerned that having a teacher spend only two years in the classroom would add to the unpredictability of the students' lives and leave them feeling abandoned. These were real and understandable concerns, and I would end up spending years grappling with them and designing a program that would address them through recruiting a diverse corps and investing a great deal not only in preservice training but also, more important, in ongoing professional development.

I could encounter ninety-nine unresponsive or critical people and feel discouraged, but just a little positive reinforcement from another person would pick me up and keep me going for a long time. A senior executive at Young & Rubicam once called me up and said, "I de-signed the advertising campaign for the Peace Corps. I just read your proposal and think that what you are trying to do is incredible. Let's meet tomorrow." Those phone calls were few and far between, but they energized me. I also got very enthusiastic responses from most school districts.

The most prevalent concern I encountered was that people didn't believe college students would want to sign up. Certain I could prove them wrong, I assembled a small team to launch a grassroots recruitment campaign and put fliers under doors at many different campuses. Twenty-five hundred people responded in four months! This resulted in media coverage and one thing led to another.

My search for the funding we needed for the first year got the boost it needed when none other than Ross Perot finally responded to one of my letters. One day I received a call from someone claiming to be him. At first, I assumed the caller was a friend playing a joke on me, but it really was Ross Perot! I could hardly breathe, let alone speak. I told him I would be in Dallas the following week and asked if we could meet. He agreed and I got off the phone and scheduled my trip.

I have never been so determined in a meeting in my life. I knew that I had no option but to leave Mr. Perot's office with the funding necessary to train and place our future corps members. As I saw it, Teach For America's fate rested on this meeting. At first, Mr. Perot suggested I contact some other philanthropists for this venture, but finally, after two hours of back and forth, he offered us a challenge grant of $500,000. We would have to match his money three to one in order to get it. This grant proved to be the catalyst we needed and it gave others the confidence to come through with the remaining funds we needed.

One year after I graduated, I was looking out on an auditorium full of Teach For America's 489 charter corps members. They were beginning their training and getting ready to begin teaching in six urban and rural communities across the country.

I tell everyone who is charting new territory or pursuing big ideas that the best way to think about getting support is to view it as a search for allies. You don't need everyone; you only need a few people who really believe in you and your ideas. So don't worry about all the nos. Stay positive and keep up the pursuit for those few yeses.

After more than fifteen years of running Teach For America, I began meeting social entrepreneurs from all over the world who were determined to launch the same model in their countries and were looking for help. Working together with the founder of a similar program in the UK, Teach First, I began envisioning a global network called Teach For All, which would seek to accelerate the impact of the model around the world. I can't tell you the number of people who advised me against this idea. They were worried that it would be a distraction and also that it wouldn't be feasible for me to lead an international network and be a good mom (by this point I had four kids). Enough people were questioning the sanity of this pursuit that I started to question it myself. One evening I had dinner with Fazle Abed, who runs BRAC, one of the largest nongovernmental organizations in the world, to seek his opinion. When I explained the doubts and asked, "Do you think I can do this?" he instanta-neously said, "Of course you can! You must!" He explained that the value I would bring to Teach For All was my experience and that I didn't need to constantly be on an airplane to impart it. Fazle's definitive advice is what solidified my decision to move forward with Teach For All.

I have come to realize how much more efficient and effective it is to unleash the leader-ship in others as opposed to doing everything myself. Teach For America began as a one-person show. We quickly became a group, then a very small team, then a much larger one. Nothing has been easy. We continue to face challenges, skeptics, and learning curves on

every front, but I am fortunate to be surrounded by a crew of people who are dedicated and deeply grounded. We keep one another going.

## WENDY'S PEARLS

■ It's essential to strike the right balance between confidence and humility. If you don't have enough confidence in the rightness of your pursuit, you'll give up too easily. But you must also have enough humility to recognize your own limitations and be receptive to learning from others. When I started Teach For America, I knew I didn't have any experience in what I was setting out to accomplish so I had a very open mind and looked for help and advice from all quarters. You have to have an ethic of continuous improvement. It's almost impossible to get anything perfect right out of the gate.

■ Be prepared for naysayers at every turn. Just look in the blogosphere and you will see many critiques of Teach For America. I try to keep myself centered on the magnitude and consequences of the problem we're addressing and in the pursuit of getting better and better at tackling it. We need more people "in the arena" working to develop creative and constructive solutions, and I feel privileged to be working alongside many others to make a meaningful impact.

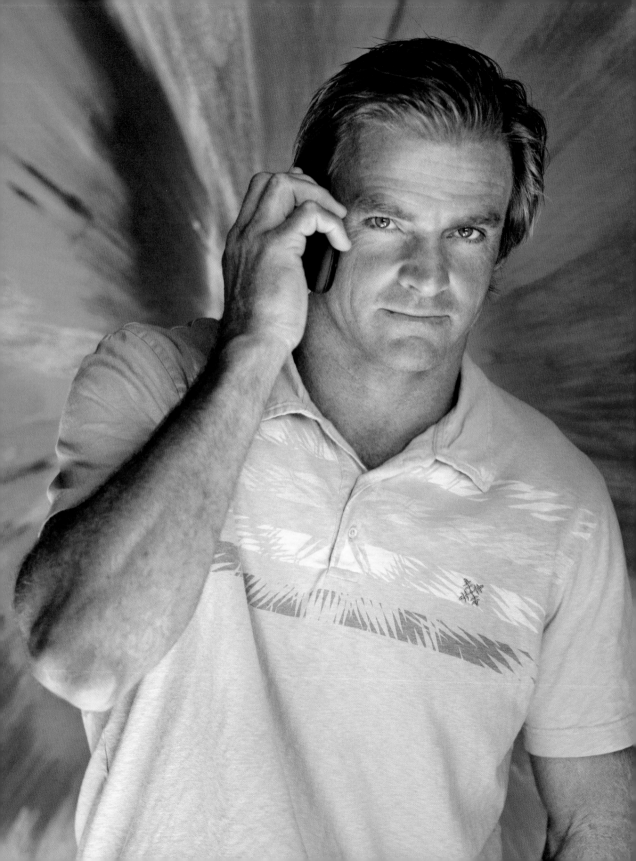

# LAIRD HAMILTON
# BIG WAVE SURFER

**MY BIOLOGICAL FATHER LEFT MY MOTHER WHEN I WAS VERY YOUNG. I NEVER KNEW HIM. MY MOM AND I MOVED TO HAWAII WHEN I WAS STILL AN INFANT. I WAS DEFINITELY** in search of a father figure, and when I was three years old, I found one at the beach. I had sneaked away from home and was playing alone in the waves when along came a popular surfer named Billy Hamilton.

He said, "Hi," and asked what I was up to. I said that I was bodysurfing, and he dove right in to join me. We befriended each other. He put me on his back and we rode little waves together. When we finished I grabbed his hand and said, "I want you to come up and meet my mom." I wanted to hook the two of them up. So he took me home, I made the introduction, and they fell in love. They were married within six months, and it wasn't long before my little brother was born.

In the beginning, Billy was my hero. I looked up to him and was so happy and proud that he was my father. But he ultimately became a disappointment. All he wanted to do was surf (which I, of all people, can understand), but he wasn't making much of a living from it and resented having to support the family. To him, it was as if it were our fault he had to work. We lived in an impoverished manner—our house was located next to a pig farm, had a tin roof, an outhouse, and no hot running water—and we ended up on welfare. Billy also had a temper that he couldn't control. I admit to being a hell-raiser as a child, but when the time came for me to be disciplined, things could get a little excessive.

As I entered my teens and grew a bit more defiant, my stepdad became very disparaging of me. He would say things like "You're never gonna be what I am." I resolved to become a lot *more* than he was. My competitive feelings continued to grow as my respect for Billy diminished. Luckily, my mom was around to instill in me a good sense of self-worth or I would

really have been in trouble. I do have a lot more sympathy for my stepfather now that I have my own kids and, ironically, I almost have to thank him for inspiring me to become both the athlete and family man I am today.

Billy wasn't the only driving force in my life, though. There was a tremendous amount of racial discrimination in Hawaii back then. White people represented the descendants of Captain James Cook and the plantation owners who, according to the natives, "destroyed" the culture of Hawaii. They called us "haoles" and were extremely resentful of our presence. When I first went to school, we were the only Caucasian family in the neighborhood. My white-blond hair caused me to stand out even more. I had no friends and was constantly ostracized and tormented. I remember being invited by a group of kids to go on a hike when I was about seven years old. I was thrilled to be included—but they ended up leading me way up into the mountains and then disappearing. They were intentionally trying to lose me, and it worked; I didn't know where I was. When I finally found my way back, they formed a human blockade to prevent me from reaching my house. I put my head down and ran right at them like an angry bull. They got out of the way.

Throughout my adolescence, I had no opportunity to date. Even if I liked a girl and she liked me, it was always "Sorry, I can't go out with you 'cause, you know, you've got blond hair." I used to lie in bed at night and wish that I would wake up as a big strong Hawaiian guy.

The ocean was the one place I found equality, so I channeled all my energy and frustrations into the water. We lived right at the Banzai Pipeline, which is probably the best place in the world for a surfer to grow up. It was the mecca of surfing, where the pioneers of big-wave riding came to challenge and prove themselves. They went out on days when everyone else was evacuated, and I looked to them for inspiration. I became known as a fearless daredevil. That and being a troublemaker in school were my ways of changing the type of attention I received. When I did something outrageous, instead of kids saying, "Wow, look at him, he's a white boy," they would say, "Wow, look at him, he's crazy!" My new identity created a safe place for me, a place where I was no longer a target.

My childhood as an outsider affected me in other ways too. I wouldn't say that I don't care what people think, but I certainly don't allow it to prevent me from doing what I want to do. I would not have survived as a kid had I not developed this mindset. It's enabled me to become an out-of-the-box thinker and innovator.

My goals are constantly evolving so I never entirely achieve them. This is actually a good thing, because once you realize your goal, then where do you go? That's your crescendo. I've seen this happen to a lot of my friends. They set a goal to be World Champion of X, or even something far more modest, and then once they attain it, they live a life of disappointment. If you don't continually revise your goals, the only place you've got to go is down. So I keep thinking of ways to reinvent wave riding.

When I cocreated tow-in surfing, a method of accessing a previously unridden realm of waves by being towed into them by a jet ski, it revolutionized the sport but it was also met with much criticism and resentment. People felt it was cheating and decried the noise and exhaust created by the engines. But we forged ahead, and before long, people started to emulate us. Today, it's widely accepted as a legitimate sport. I continue to run into a lot of resistance whenever I innovate, but having experienced this kind of confirmation enables me to get through it.

There are two somewhat related mottos that I literally live by. The first is an old aviation saying, but it applies to any potentially dangerous field: "There are old pilots and there are bold pilots; but there are no old bold pilots." Fearing perilous situations is intelligent. Humans would never have survived without this characteristic. I try to understand my fear and use it to make good decisions. If you want to stick around, you have to be cautious. Which leads me to my next saying, and I made this one up myself: "Potato chips in is potato chips out." Sounds funny, I know, but it means that what you put into something is *exactly* what you can expect to get out of it. Although my mother had a great work ethic, there's been no person—or thing—that's taught me this more often and deeply than the ocean. I've been sucked out to sea and pounded by waves many times after already being exhausted from hours of surfing. If I get too tired before I'm able to make my escape, I'm going to drown. There's no room for slackers in my field. A large part of being cautious means being extremely prepared, both mentally and physically. I put in hours upon hours of strength and endurance training. I also make it my business to understand everything I can about the environment I am working in and only partner with people I have complete faith in.

While I may still look like the daredevil of my youth, the risks I take today are extremely calculated. And although parts of my life have been tough, I wouldn't change any of it if it meant not being the person I am today.

## LAIRD'S PEARL

■ I am frequently asked if getting married and having children (I have three daughters) has changed my behavior. The answer is, "not in the water." It is essential to have the support of the person you are in a relationship with. If your partner prevents you from fulfilling your potential, it's not good for anybody. My wife understands what I do and knows that continuing along the path I'm on is part of what I need to be happy. I also feel that it's important for my daughters to know the real me—the guy who comes in from riding giant waves and has that look in his eye. I want them to see what it does for me so that perhaps one day they can find the thing that gives them that feeling.

# MUHAMMAD YUNUS
# NOBEL PEACE PRIZE RECIPIENT

**I WAS BORN IN CHITTAGONG, A PORT CITY IN BANGLADESH, IN 1940. WE WERE A VERY MODEST, LOW-INCOME FAMILY AND LIVED ON A BUSY STREET IN THE HEART OF TOWN** above my father's jewelry shop. My parents were devout Muslims and hard workers, but they were largely uneducated. My father went to school through eighth grade and my mother only through fourth. They had fourteen children, five of whom died very young.

My father could have used some of us to help with his business, but his priority was to make sure we all went to college. He was strict about our need to study. My parents certainly believed in me, but I don't think either of them could have imagined that I would grow up to start a bank—especially one that revolutionized lending in the developing world.

I did well in school and went on to study economics at a Bangladeshi university. In 1965 I received a Fulbright Scholarship to study in the United States, where I obtained a PhD in economic development from Vanderbilt University. In 1971 I returned to Bangladesh where I became a professor and head of the department of economics at the University of Chittagong.

At the time, Bangladesh was in a terrible state. It had been through a war and had just become an independent country (prior to 1971, Bangladesh was part of Pakistan). The economy was shattered and sliding downhill fast. On top of that, there was a great famine in 1974. Thousands of people were roaming the streets hungry, dying of starvation.

I used to get a thrill from standing in a classroom and teaching elegant economic theories, but I started to dread my own lectures. Nothing I taught accurately reflected the horrors around me. What good was I doing for the people suffering on my doorstep? In great agony, I resolved to find a way to help.

I decided to start going to Jobra, the village next to the university's campus, every day to see if I could make myself useful to the people living there. I brought my students with me. We got to know the residents and came face-to-face with their struggle to eke out a living. In many cases, they needed only the tiniest amount of money to support their efforts, but their only option was to borrow from ruthless loan sharks whose usurious terms transformed them into virtual slaves. We found forty-two people trapped in a cycle of poverty by these moneylenders. Shockingly enough, the total amount of money needed to release all forty-two of them from their servitude was the equivalent of twenty-seven U.S. dollars.

We learned that for people living on pennies a day just a few dollars could transform their lives. I reached into my own pocket and lent them the money. The excitement and gratitude they showed in response to this gesture touched me deeply. I thought, *If this small action makes so many people so happy, I should do more of it*. But rather than lend money on an ad hoc basis, I wanted to create an institutional answer these people could rely on.

I visited the local bank and tried hard to persuade them to start making loans to the villagers, but they refused, stating that the poor were not creditworthy. For several months I met with increasingly senior bank officials, but I couldn't change their minds. Finally, I proposed personally guaranteeing loans to the poor. It was my only option, but I also believed that my borrowers would repay the loans. After much deliberation and hesitation, the bank agreed—although they called me idealistic and told me to say good-bye to my money.

By the middle of 1976 I was acting as an informal banker, lending money to the poor for the specific purpose of allowing them to create entrepreneurial income-generating opportunities, such as farming and manufacturing goods to sell. The recipients knew that this was their only opportunity to break out of poverty and they paid every one of the loans back on time.

The bank officials felt it was just luck and warned me that I would never be able to succeed on a larger scale—but I expanded to two villages, then three, and the program continued to grow. It started to become apparent that serving the poor's financial needs could be a sustainable business. I kept trying to persuade the bank to lend to them without me as the guarantor, but I couldn't change their minds. Instead, the bank officials warned me that my structure would eventually collapse. I responded, "Until it does, I am going to keep doing it."

I finally decided to create a separate bank to serve the needs of the poor. It was a long, arduous process but I was able to get it done in 1983. We named it Grameen Bank, which is Bengali for "Village Bank." The kind of banking we did became known as "microcredit" or "microfinance" because our loans were so small. Our plan was to charge interest on the loans and have all profits go to the borrowers, who would be the owners of the bank.

Knowing very little about running a bank, I had to start from scratch. Using mostly common sense and my intuition, I made up most of the rules as I went along, but I also decided to study the existing banking system to see which of its methods we could use. Because Grameen was pursuing a different kind of borrower than the traditional banks were, we ended up with a fundamentally different approach. The banks demanded lump-sum repayments. We instituted a weekly repayment program (parting with a large sum of cash could be psychologically trying for borrowers and often caused them to default—with our weekly method, the loan payments were so small that the borrowers barely missed the money). Banks conducted their business primarily in city centers. We went to the small villages where our borrowers lived. Banks did not lend to women. We set an initial goal of having half our borrowers be women. Banks required collateral for their loans and wanted to know as much as they could about a person's past before lending. We didn't require collateral and were more interested in the future prospects of our borrowers.

I believe that poverty is created by society and is not a reflection on the poor themselves. There is nothing wrong with them. They are not destitute and illiterate because they are stupid or lazy—they were just born into a life where there was no formal financial structure available to help them succeed. Grameen was founded to give these people the break they needed to start fresh and unleash their potential.

Surprisingly enough, it was difficult to convince people to borrow from us at first. What we were doing was so unconventional that we were met with a lot of skepticism and fear. In Islam, the primary religion in Bangladesh, charging interest is not acceptable and neither is lending money to women who, according to rural clerics' views, are not supposed to be involved in any business. People started saying that Grameen was un-Islamic. Contradicting a religion provokes a lot of very emotional, aggressive responses. In addition, the existing moneylenders saw us as a danger to their business.

Rumors circulated that we were, among other things, communists trying to organize the poor, "blood suckers" exploiting the poor, and missionaries in disguise whose real purpose was to convert the poor to Christianity. Men were especially against us because our efforts tended to empower women. Feeling threatened and insulted, they tried to frighten off women by saying that if they took a loan from us they would be banished from society, attacked, or even thrown into the deep sea. Women not only worried about creating problems for their families but were also insecure about handling money. Most of them had never touched it before and had been told their whole lives that they were good for nothing.

It required a lot of patience and determination, but we didn't give up. We continued to calmly explain ourselves and attempted to build the confidence of our borrowers—especially the women. We had to convince them to see value in themselves and that they didn't need rank or status to advance their stations in life. It took six years before we reached our initial goal of women making up fifty percent of our borrowers, but along the way something interesting happened. We observed that when money entered a family through women it went

toward purchases that benefited children and the household in general, while most men tended to focus on their own personal needs. We concluded that females had more drive to overcome poverty and lending to them brought about the most rapid change for the entire society. As a result, we began to concentrate on lending to women. Today, ninety-seven percent of Grameen borrowers are women.

I believe that all human beings are capable of being entrepreneurs. In order to demonstrate this, Grameen began lending money to beggars. We said, "As you go from house to house begging, would you like to carry some merchandise with you to sell? This will not require doing extra work; you'll just be giving people more options." We reasoned that if the beggars succeeded in paying us back from the business they did it would show that even the poorest people on earth could be entrepreneurs. We predicted that there would be one or two thousand beggars in the program, but we ended up with more than one hundred thousand. Within five years, more than twenty-two thousand people stopped begging and became, among other things, successful door-to-door salespeople and personal shoppers for housewives.

We opened Grameen branches throughout the country, and today the bank has more than 8.5 million borrowers and makes more than $1.5 billion of new loans each year. In addition, the concept of microfinance has spread around the world, including industrialized countries, and has helped millions more. Creating Grameen and the microfinance movement has been immensely fulfilling and gave me the confidence that I could accomplish many more things.

Working so closely with the poor gave me an inside view of the various issues, beyond a lack of credit, that they struggle with. Whenever I see a problem, my instinct is to create a business to fix it. As a result, I've created about fifty companies over the years. Almost all, like Grameen Bank, exist for the sole purpose of helping others. Some got off the ground with little effort, while others were far more difficult to create. For example, because many of my borrowers didn't have access to electricity, I created a home solar-energy-system company. A lot of people didn't think this business would work in Bangladesh, but I had to try. In the beginning it was a huge struggle to sell even five solar home systems per month, but after fifteen years, we were selling more than a thousand per day! We'll soon have 1.5 million homes in Bangladesh enjoying solar home systems.

We later began partnering with multinational companies to create businesses. In 2007, for example, we partnered with Groupe Danone to produce yogurt fortified with micronutrients for malnourished children. We then collaborated with Veolia Environment to bring affordable clean water to the villages, Adidas to make affordable shoes, and BASF to create chemically treated nets that protect people from insect-born diseases such as malaria.

I began to call these types of ventures "social businesses." The money used to create them is paid back to the investor, but all profit after that is put back into the company.

Instead of measuring success by how much money is made, the success of social businesses is measured by how much of a positive social impact is made.

In March 2011 the government of Bangladesh forced me to resign from Grameen Bank, their reason being that I was more than sixty years old. It was politically motivated and very upsetting, but it didn't deter me from continuing along my path. That same year, I co-founded Yunus Social Business, an organization dedicated to empowering and promoting social businesses in many countries on all continents.

Human creativity is limitless. If we channel it toward addressing the problems we have created over the years, we can redesign anything and construct the kind of world in which we want to live. And you don't have to start big. If what you do improves the lives of only five people, it's worth it. I always remember that I started my own journey by making personal loans of only twenty-seven dollars to a small group of villagers.

## MUHAMMAD'S PEARLS

■ If you observe something that bothers you, make your own action plan to fix it. There are many things that have been designed in the wrong way. Don't take existing theories for granted. Don't think that other people know more than you or that everything has been done. Your theory may be right and you can become the new expert. I made up my own rules of banking and they worked.

■ People often respond to something new and unusual in a negative way. Be prepared for this. As long as you are convinced that what you are doing is right, go ahead and do it!

# RACHEL ZOE
# STYLIST/FASHION DESIGNER

**THERE WAS A MOMENT IN TIME WHEN I THOUGHT I'D BE A RESTAURANT HOSTESS FOR THE REST OF MY LIFE. I HAD THAT JOB DURING THE SUMMERS WHEN I WAS IN HIGH** school and when I was at George Washington University. I thought it was the coolest job because I loved meeting new people every day. That's actually how I met my husband, Rodger. He was getting his MBA at the time, but he was also employed as a waiter where I worked. We fell in love and I fantasized that we'd open a restaurant together some day, but he had his sights set on a career in finance.

When I graduated from college, I had no idea what I wanted to do and went to my grandfather for advice. He said, "Do whatever it is that you love and success will come." He was so wise. That theory had held true for me as a student. If I wasn't interested in a subject (anything involving numbers literally gave me nightmares), I struggled. It was as if my brain had shut down. Conversely, when I loved something, such as psychology and sociology, I was great at it. I truly believe that if you are not passionate about something you probably won't succeed at it because you won't be driven to get up every day and work hard. I wanted to discover a career that I was excited about instead of one I felt I had to do.

I had always been in love with fashion. As a little girl, I was perpetually overdressed for everything and about five years ahead of the trend. When I got older, I was constantly doing everyone's hair and makeup. So, through a friend of a friend's sister, I was able to land a job as a fashion assistant at *YM*, a teen magazine, in New York City. I didn't even know what a fashion assistant was, but I figured that if it contained the word "fashion" it was where I was meant to be.

I learned so much at *YM* and truly loved what I was doing—producing and styling fashion shoots for the magazine—but at the same time it proved to be a real challenge. My boss made a habit of stealing the clothing we had access to and then falsely accusing me. We were in a continual battle, and as a result, it was a constant emotional struggle. Rodger, who was working like crazy as an investment banker at the time, would have to cheerlead and console me around the clock. He'd say, "Baby, you just have to keep going. What goes around comes around. There will be karma." I didn't think so—but one day my boss and I were on a photo shoot in Miami and the fashion director (my boss's superior) caught her stealing red-handed. She was fired on the spot, and I was given her job as senior fashion editor. It was amazing!

The fashion director then sat me down for a serious talk. She told me that in order to succeed in this industry I had to grow thicker skin and stop being so nice. The talk was discouraging and made me question my career choice for a while, but eventually I came to the conclusion that I didn't agree with everything she said. I did need to toughen up, and surviving the hardships with my boss made me realize that, but I believe people can be strong and nice at the same time. My father is the nicest person I've ever known and he has served as the CEO and president of several companies throughout his career.

My job at *YM* sent me all over the world, and I got to meet a lot of celebrities and models. I was working incredibly hard, but even though I was promoted to senior fashion editor within two years I was still only earning a small salary. I took stock of my situation and decided I'd be better off leaving my job to freelance as a stylist. Everyone asked, "Do you have any clients lined up?" I didn't. My plan was to work as hard as I could and make it happen.

I had made some connections with publicists, talent agents, and managers while working at *YM*. When I told them I was going freelance, they said, "You're hired." I started styling big music stars like the Backstreet Boys, Enrique Iglesias, Jessica Simpson, and Britney Spears, while also freelancing as a contributing editor for a number of fashion magazines. I was a one-woman show and working around the clock. I was on a plane every other day, traveling with ten trunks of clothes. It was extremely exhausting, but I loved being on my own and finally making a decent income.

Work frequently brought me to Los Angeles, sometimes for a month at a time. Eventually, Rodger and I decided to move there. Back then, the fashion scene in Hollywood was very different than it is today. The fashion world was not interested in Hollywood, and Hollywood, in turn, was intimidated by fashion. The red carpet, for example, hadn't yet become the place to showcase truly amazing fashion moments. But I didn't see why these two worlds couldn't be more integrated.

Through my freelance work, I met Jennifer Garner's publicist, and she hired me to style Jen for the Emmys at the last minute. This was my first big job working with an actress and her being seen in the glamorous look I selected changed everything for me. Shortly thereafter, I transitioned into styling actresses and began working with Cameron Diaz, Kate Hudson, and Keira Knightley. I felt so lucky to be dressing such talented, beautiful women in haute couture. I also started meeting all of the fashion designers I had always idolized from a distance. I couldn't believe this was my job—but I don't want to totally sugarcoat it. While I may have been attending movie premieres and hanging out with celebrities, I was there to fluff my clients' trains, hold their handbags, and make sure they had ChapStick, lint brushes, and snacks on hand. I was there to provide a service and never lost sight of that.

I took chances and sent my clients out in looks that were unexpected and sometimes even slightly controversial. Fortunately, the response was mostly great. When it wasn't, I had to remind myself that both the client and I were happy and confident with the look and that's really all that mattered. If you don't take chances, then what's the fun in playing the game?

At the time, publications started to focus on candidly photographing celebrities during their down time, so I began dressing my clients for their daily life too. If they were going to be photographed getting coffee in the morning, why not do it in a great outfit? My clients began getting positive feedback on what they wore and everything snowballed from there.

I still work as a stylist but I have moved on to expand my business. In 2011 I launched my eponymous contemporary collection, including ready-to-wear, footwear, and jewelry. I've also published two books, was the executive producer and star of my own television show, and started a digital media company and online style destination, the Zoe Report.

I never made a blueprint for my future and don't believe in setting rigid career goals. Career paths usually require a lot of trial and error, and you have to allow yourself the freedom to go with the flow. Sometimes you think you should go in one direction, but it doesn't work out or feel right. Occasionally, a better opportunity presents itself and you start over in a different area. If you set a goal that isn't fairly realistic, you could be setting yourself up for failure—which can really set you back emotionally.

All businesses are competitive, but people in the fashion and entertainment industries can be especially catty and vindictive. In those worlds your social and professional lives are intertwined and there are a lot of superficialities involved. It often feels as though you were back in junior high school. It can be ruthless.

I was very naïve when I started and had a hard time figuring out whom to trust. There were many instances where people who I had considered friends turned out not to be. It's been a constant learning curve, and I now have my eyes and ears open all the time. I'm far less naïve than before, but I am in a continual battle to not become cynical. I try to put blinders on, stay focused, be great at my job, and keep looking toward the future. There are enough clients and business opportunities out there for everybody. If you get too wrapped up in what your competition is doing, you'll just trip yourself up.

Rodger has become my business partner—he's my best friend in the world and ensures

that I am surrounded by a team of honest, kind, and loyal people. We've found that those characteristics are the most important to look for—everything else can be learned on the job. When you find great employees, you must let them know how much you value them and hold on tight. My team is like family to me. It took a long time for me to have the confidence to relinquish control, trust, and even rely on other people.

Of all of the roles I've ever taken on, becoming a mother has had the largest impact on me. It has given me a new, healthier set of priorities. I used to be very focused on myself and would spend the majority of my time thinking, *How can I be better? How can I work harder?* My career consumed and ran my life. When something went wrong, I would let it affect me too much—even petty, insignificant things. When my first son was born, it was as if a new life started for me too. I now have two sons and spend my time wondering how I can make their lives the best for them. Petty things can still upset me, but only for a very short time now. Then I look at my kids and realize, *It does not matter.* Negativity burns inside of you and keeps you awake at night. If you can avoid letting it consume you, I strongly suggest doing so. You will have more freedom to enjoy life and focus on important, productive things.

## RACHEL'S PEARLS

■   Be prepared to work hard for everything you want. Nothing is easy—and when something appears to be, there's usually a lot of work that's gone on behind the scenes. I sat next to an editor in chief of one of the biggest magazines in the world at a fashion show in Milan a few years ago. She said, "I feel like you just sort of came about. All of a sudden you're sitting front row, next to me, at all of these shows." I looked at her and thought, *Just came about? I have been working like crazy for the last fifteen years!*

■   The media can be a huge obstacle for many people. One day they will print the nastiest lies and then the next day they'll be nice and supportive. When this first happened to me, I wanted to stand at the top of Mount Everest and scream, "This is not okay!" But the crazy thing is that most of the time there's not much you can do. Eventually, I stopped reading about myself. I know who I am and the people in my life, including my clients, do too.

■   I never had formal training, but if you know you want to be a fashion designer, go to fashion school. Being skilled in the technical aspects of your trade can only help you. I would love to be able to sit down and actually make an incredible couture dress myself. Instead, I sketch it on a piece of paper and then depend on other people to execute it. There is definitely more room for error and more work involved in doing it this way.

# JEFF KINNEY
# DIARY OF A WIMPY KID AUTHOR

**I WAS BORN ON AN AIR FORCE BASE IN MARYLAND AND GREW UP IN A SUBURB OF WASHINGTON, D.C. MY FATHER WAS A DISCIPLINED MILITARY MAN.** He did two tours in Vietnam then worked as an analyst at the Pentagon. But in his private time he collected comic books—and fostered a real love of them in me.

Influenced by my dad, I went to Villanova University on a military scholarship with the intention of eventually joining the U.S. Air Force. While there, I created a comic strip called *Igdoof* about a socially maladjusted freshman and was able to get it into the school's newspaper. I had found my calling—and at the same time I realized I wasn't suited for the military. I was born to be a cartoonist. I dropped out of Villanova after a year and transferred to the University of Maryland.

It felt like a regressive step at the time because I was losing my full ride to college and going home with my tail between my legs, but I found that Maryland was the perfect school for me. They had a daily newspaper (which was somewhat rare in colleges) with a readership of between 30,000 and 50,000 students, and after a couple of failed attempts, I was able to get *Igdoof* into it. It was a great place to cut my teeth and develop my cartooning abilities. I thought that I would be able to take it right into the grown-up world of syndicated newspapers, however I was realistic enough to know I needed a backup plan to pay the bills and decided to pursue a degree in computer science. But I soon discovered that my cartoons took priority over everything else. I knew that just one professor would read any term paper I wrote, whereas my next *Igdoof* cartoon would be read by tens of thousands of people. Three and a half years into my computer science degree, I was close to being kicked out of the program.

During school breaks, I interned at the Bureau of Alcohol, Tobacco, and Firearms (ATF). When it became apparent that I wasn't going to make it in the computer science department, I decided to switch my major to criminal justice and set my sights on becoming an ATF agent.

Right when I was about to graduate, the siege and destruction of the Branch Davidian compound in Waco, Texas, occurred. The ATF was heavily involved. Four ATF officers were killed and sixteen were wounded. As a result, they had a hiring freeze. Forced to go in a totally different direction, I got a job doing graphics and headline writing for a paper in Massachusetts, then moved on to a medical software company, and eventually landed as a games designer at FunBrain, a website offering educational games for children.

All the while, I continued to pursue my newspaper-cartooning career. I would spend between six and nine months putting together a submission packet and then send it out to all the syndicates—only to get really tough, terse rejection letters back. This went on for a few years and it was very soul sucking. It's hard to send your best work out there and get no encouragement whatsoever. I even read a book on how to get syndicated and tried to learn from that, but to no avail. I finally came to terms with the fact that it was a waste of time to keep sending out submissions. My illustrations just weren't professional grade—my skill level had topped out at that of a middle school kid, and I knew it. Accepting this fact was tough but at the same time very liberating. It's what eventually allowed me to have my big moment.

I realized that if I drew like a kid I should embrace it and stop trying to draw like an adult—and also that because newspapers wouldn't accept my work I had to find another medium that would. At the time, I was keeping a journal filled with sketches. I decided to try writing a fictional story in that format. It would be a book written in handwriting from a kid's perspective with cartoon drawings interspersed throughout.

I came up with the title *Diary of a Wimpy Kid* right away. It seemed a little provocative, which I hoped would serve to grab people's attention. In my mind, it would be a book for adults that reminded them of what it was like to be a kid. I felt as if this was going to be my opus, my one good idea, so I didn't impose any deadline on myself to finish it—but, quite frankly, I thought I'd be done in a month or two.

At first, I was writing too quickly, and a lot of the material I came up with wasn't very funny. I decided that before I started writing the actual book I would come up with seventy-seven "idea pages" in a sketchbook. From those, I would then include only the best ones. It ended up taking me four years to fill up my seventy-seven idea pages. It took another four years after that before I even finished the first draft. I kept working and reworking my jokes and characters. It ended up being about eight years between the time I conceived of the project and when I finally had something in hand that I actually wanted to show anyone.

There were a few things that kept me going and allowed me to be patient during those eight years: In the fifth grade I had a teacher named Mrs. Norton who was probably in her seventies. She was a stout, matronly kind of woman. Not the kind of person you would think might inspire a young boy, but she was very instrumental in my development as a writer and artist. For years I had been drawing pictures, showing them to relatives and friends, and getting nothing but praise. One day in school I was drawing a picture of a woman and began to run out of room at the bottom of the page—so I shortened her legs so her feet would fit. Mrs. Norton took a look at my drawing and, recognizing that I had talent, challenged me to do better. She chided me for not planning things out and for sort of cheating at the end and trying to get away with it. I'll never forget that. It was a lesson on the importance of planning ahead, but more significant, it was a lesson in embracing excellence and not accepting praise for something that I knew wasn't great. Mrs. Norton taught me that it's better to not put anything out there than to put something out that's mediocre.

There was also the billboard that I used to drive by on my way to work every day. On it was the Benjamin Franklin quote, "Well done is better than well said." Don't even ask me who paid to have it put up, but I felt as if it were speaking right to me. People often broadcast their goals then get embarrassed if they are unable to deliver. When you announce your intentions, you become trapped by them. Adding social pressure to your situation gives you less flexibility. I knew I was working on something special and protected myself by telling only a very few people about it. Also, since I was so used to rejection, I was pretty much expecting it once I submitted my material. As long as I continued working on the project, I could hold on to the fantasy that it might actually be published one day. As a result, part of me wasn't in any real rush to finish up quickly and shop my book around.

In 2004 FunBrain was looking for something to put on their site that would entice users to return regularly during the long summer holidays. I showed my boss some of my *Wimpy Kid* work, and we began posting it in the form of short daily diary entries. The work soon had an audience of millions.

A couple of publishers had heard through the grapevine that I wanted my comic to become a book, checked it out online, and sent me preemptive rejection letters. It was like having the prettiest girl at school walk up to you to say that she didn't want to go to prom with you *before* you even asked her. Although the material that was online at the time was about ninety percent similar to what ended up in the book, I continued to work on it for at least a year and a half after that.

One day in 2006 my boss told me that a comics convention, Comic Con, was coming up in New York and encouraged me to go there to look for talent for our website. He also suggested I use the opportunity to look for a publisher for *Diary of a Wimpy Kid*. I went to Kinko's, printed out a few sample packets containing about twenty pages of my book, and headed to the convention. Unfortunately, Comic Con had oversold tickets that year. I waited in line for hours but was turned away. I was about to go back home (I was living with my wife in Massachusetts at that point), but I had heard that Billy Joel was playing Madison Square Garden, and although the show was supposedly sold out, I decided to go to the box

office and try my luck. They had one ticket left! I called my wife and asked her how she'd feel about my spending the night in the city and going to the concert (our finances were pretty tight at the time and the cost of a New York City hotel and a concert ticket was not inconsequential to us). She said, "Sure, go ahead and stay." I did, then I decided to return to Comic Con the next morning and I was able to get in.

I walked up and down the aisles talking to different publishers, trying to get a feel for things. Most people were not interested in my work and others told me that a convention wasn't the right forum for submissions. One editor mentioned that Abrams had recently turned a web comic called *Mom's Cancer* into a book. I noted that and continued walking around the convention floor. On my very last aisle, I saw *Mom's Cancer* in one of the booths and stopped in my tracks. An Abrams editor, Charlie Kochman, was standing in the booth, took notice of my interest, and wanted to sell me a book. I browsed through it and gladly gave him $12.95, figuring it was my entry fee to talk to him. What transpired from that point on was almost like a miracle. I asked Charlie if he would be willing to take a look at *Diary of a Wimpy Kid* and pulled out one of my packets. I don't know if he actually read any of it, but he looked at the pages and said, "This is exactly what we're looking for. It's the reason we came here." (It was Abrams' first Comic Con too!) We exchanged information and parted ways. It was really exciting. I felt as if something momentous had just occurred. Charlie felt the same way. He said he photographed the moment in his mind because he knew this was going to be something really special.

Abrams held on to my submission for several months. I made it through one or two hurdles (the editorial board and the publication board liked my work) but there were some people at the company who weren't so sure about it. Charlie kept me apprised of every development. I was very anxious and spent this whole waiting period experiencing insomnia (which I had never experienced before). Charlie eventually called and told me that Abrams wanted to make *Diary of a Wimpy Kid* into a series, but that it was going to be for kids. That part was really jarring. In my opinion, the enjoyment of my book was predicated on the capacity to recognize irony, which I felt was too sophisticated a concept for kids. I thought Abrams was overestimating kids' ability to understand that style of humor. But within a short amount of time, I realized that my writing was more or less G-rated anyway and I convinced myself that it would work. As it turned out, I was underestimating kids—they do understand the book.

Knowing that I was going to be a published author was very exciting and scary at the same time. In April 2007 a print run of 15,000 *Diary of a Wimpy Kid* books was published. Its immediate success took everyone by surprise. I have now completed the first nine of what is supposed to be a ten-book series. There are currently more than 150 million *Diary of a Wimpy Kid* books in print and three of them have been made into movies.

I still write each book with an adult audience in mind. I am afraid that if I picture a child audience I'll start to write down to them and moralize. I like to keep my books pretty much lesson free. I see them as joke delivery mechanisms. I'm a gag writer, and I'm just trying to keep kids entertained. If there is a lesson baked in, it's that reading can be fun. If my books turn kids on to reading, I feel very proud of that.

I still work very slowly and deliberately. These days it takes me about nine months to create a book from start to finish. During crunch time, I work an average of about fifteen hours per day—for two months at a time. It's very intense. Unfortunately, when it comes to writing, putting a lot of time in does not always guarantee that a quality product will come out. Sometimes I'll sit for four hours at a time and not be able to come up with anything worthwhile. I'll often fall asleep feeling depressed and frustrated. Inevitably, there are periods of time when I feel that the book I'm working on is, quality wise, several steps below the last one and I become filled with doubt and self-loathing. It's always a real struggle, but I usually end up being pretty pleased with the result. The process takes care of the quality.

Despite having achieved some success, I still have my day job as the creative director of Poptropica, an educational gaming site for children that I conceived and set up for the company that owns FunBrain. My whole life has been about creating an audience. Through Poptropica, I reach about six million kids a month, and through *Diary of a Wimpy Kid*, I reach many, many more. Having this kind of audience is a privilege, and I want to make sure to take advantage of the opportunity while it lasts because, logically speaking, I can't stay on this track forever. Eventually, it will drop off in some fashion and I'm trying to prepare myself for that. I hope that I'll find another ten-year project when it does.

## JEFF'S PEARLS

■  You don't need to have a huge new idea to be a success. *Diary of a Wimpy Kid* is about a regular boy in middle school. I think that the best and most humorous stories come from slice-of-life everyday experiences. This is why stand-up comedy works—because people talk about the humor of everyday life and the experiences we have in common. It's also why the Judy Blume books that came out in the sixties and seventies are still relevant today. The characters are strong and the situations are relatable.

■  If you have an idea that you think is a winner, nurture it and take your time developing it. Anything worth having requires working hard. People want to jump into something and be a success right out of the gate, but becoming really good at anything that requires skill usually takes years. Whether you're an athlete, a doctor, or a writer, you have to put in a lot of effort to become an expert in your chosen field. If you do, when your opportunity finally arises, you'll be in a good position to take full advantage of it.

# JEFF KOONS
## ARTIST

**MY SISTER, KAREN, IS THREE YEARS OLDER THAN I AM AND COULD ALWAYS DO EVERYTHING BETTER. SHE COULD JUMP HIGHER, COUNT HIGHER, AND RUN FASTER.** I remember sitting at a desk at home when I was about four years old and making a drawing that my parents thought was fantastic. I finally felt as if I had a sense of place in the family— something to help give me confidence.

My parents were very encouraging, and when I turned seven, they signed me up for private art lessons. My father, an interior decorator, had a furniture store in our hometown of York, Pennsylvania. He would frame my paintings, hang them in the window, and sell them.

I was brought up to always be self-reliant. I took guitar lessons after school, and the studio I went to held a fund-raising campaign with the students selling mints door-to-door. I really enjoyed the process and was quite good at it. When the campaign was over, I decided to continue on my own. I would buy various goods—candies, gift-wrapping paper, bows, ribbons, and cards—from the back of magazines and then sell them in my neighborhood. I was extremely committed and would go out for an hour and a half every night. When I got older, I started vending soft drinks on a local golf course. I would fill up a big jug of soda and carry nice cups and towels. Sometimes I had to wait a very long time for people to come by. Selling is kind of like fishing: To be successful, you have to be persistent and patient. It felt great to do well and being a good salesman is definitely a useful skill, but what I enjoyed most was communicating and interacting with people.

Throughout high school, I never really understood how most of the subjects I studied could benefit me. As a result, I tried to just get by and pass. But I did love art class. Every study period or bit of free time I had would be spent in the art room. When it came time to graduate, I had no desire to study liberal arts in college. The only thing I was prepared for was art school, so I enrolled in the Maryland Institute College of Art (MICA) in Baltimore.

In my first art history class, the teacher showed us pictures of Manet's *Olympia*. He pointed out that different images were actually symbols and explained how they connected

153

to sociology, psychology, philosophy, and all these other areas. That's when I began to understand art's vast potential—until then, I thought it was just a way of creating a two- or three-dimensional image. I realized art could provide a way for me to expand my parameters and be involved, a little bit, in many disciplines. I had a great desire to participate in that kind of dialogue.

During my junior year at MICA, my girlfriend of just a few months became pregnant. I offered to marry her but she felt we were too young, so our daughter, Shannon, was put up for adoption. It was a terrible experience. I always wanted Shannon to be able to find me if she wanted to when she came of age, and I felt that my having greater visibility would make it easier for her. That kind of inspired me to become famous.

Remaining in Maryland proved to be very painful after Shannon's adoption. I felt that changing environments might help. I had become interested in the work of two Chicago-based artists, Jim Nutt and Ed Paschke, so I decided to take advantage of MICA's student mobility program and enroll in the School of the Art Institute of Chicago for my last year.

On my first night in Chicago, I went to a bar and in walked this tall man. I thought, *That has to be Ed Paschke*. It was. Ed and I became close friends, and I began to work as his studio assistant, stretching canvases and doing other things. I loved spending time with him and learned a tremendous amount. Ed was very ambitious and taught me about the politics of art. He continually positioned himself to take advantage of as many opportunities as possible. For example, he surrounded himself with people who shared an interest in his type of art and attended parties and events in the hopes of making connections that could be of assistance to his career. Ed also taught me about readymades (where ordinary, already made objects are displayed as art), particularly Duchamp's work. Ed got his own source material from the real world and explained, "Everything is all here. You just have to look for it." That had a huge impact on me.

After graduation, I got a job as a preparator (someone who installs artworks for exhibitions) at Chicago's Museum of Contemporary Art. Chicago was nice but a little isolating. After about a year, I decided to move to New York. I hitchhiked there with the intention of getting a preparator job at the Museum of Modern Art, but there were no positions available. I started calling every day, inquiring if anything had opened up. Finally, seeing how determined I was, they offered me a job selling tickets at the ticket booth. I took it. Selling tickets became kind of a performance for me. I would dress up a little bit every morning, wearing things such as polka-dot shirts, reflective cuff links, and double ties (a regular tie with a bow tie cut out of a sponge or something underneath). I enjoyed interacting with people and definitely got noticed.

I loved being around the museum's collection all day long and got to know it very well. Eventually, during my breaks from the ticket booth, they would let me stand behind the information desk and answer people's questions—where a certain painting was located, what time a certain movie was showing, that kind of thing. The membership desk happened to be located in the same area and I observed that the museum was doing very little to increase enrollment. People would come up to the desk, say they wanted to renew, and were handed a form. That's it. I thought the museum could be a little more aggressive in trying to get their members to upgrade. For instance, the membership desk could ask, "What kind of a membership do you have? Have you ever thought about increasing to the next level?" So I ended up switching to that desk and significantly increased the museum's membership. One day a man I had just upgraded said, "Jeff, you were able to make me a patron of the Museum of Modern Art. Why don't you come to work for me as a stockbroker?"

I took him up on his offer and began by going door-to-door selling mutual funds. Eventually, I switched to trading stocks and commodities. I was always an artist and really only wanted to be a member of the art world, but this job allowed me to be independent and produce the artwork I wanted (expensive, large-scale pieces) without being reliant on the mercy of art dealers. Sometimes I even created pieces that cost more than they sold for.

Following Ed Paschke's example, I began to immerse myself in a community of people— friends, artists, critics, gallery owners—who shared my artistic interests and I tried to say yes to every invitation that might give me an opportunity to network. I would show my work to anyone who would look and never refused an opportunity to be in a group show or to have my work exposed in any manner.

I wanted to work with readymades and produce a body of work so powerful that people would almost have a physical or chemical reaction to it. I created a series called *The New* where I encased vacuum cleaners inside clear fluorescent-lit Plexiglas—the association with the Hoover salesman going door-to-door resonated with me. The New Museum of Contemporary Art was very interested in what the possibilities of contemporary painting and sculpture could be and in 1980 they offered to display my pieces in their window on Fourteenth Street and Fifth Avenue. I consider that my first solo show, and the first piece of artwork I sold after art school was one of those vacuum cleaners. It was purchased by Patrick Lannan, a patron of the arts and a former Hoover salesman. The show helped me gain recognition and I moved forward creating other series of work. By about 1985, I reached the point where I could give up having a second job and do nothing but focus on my art.

My father was a perfectionist. When he designed interiors, he would plan out every detail before executing a thing. I picked up that quality from him. I have a vision of what I want my art to be and contemplate every detail long before I start working on it. Once I commit to making something, I am determined to produce my mental image to the best of my ability. I am as precise as possible and enjoy pushing myself to my limit. When I was younger, I would stay up for a couple of months straight working on exhibitions, frequently losing my voice.

I find a kind of ease in having a plan and sticking to it, even when I follow something as simple as a diet.

I now work out of a studio where I employ about 130 people. I have people managing the front office, people who help me work on computers, people who do painting, and people who do sculpture. My assistants make the actual works—but it's not as if I tell them to go off and make something and then sign it. I have developed a meticulous color-coded system that a team of assistants can use to execute a piece as if it's been done by a single hand—mine. I manage and control every gesture they make and there is no room for interpretation. Every distinct shade of paint is mapped out and given a number. No paint even leaves the coloring table before being approved. The way the paint is applied is controlled too. When I use this method, each painting takes between a year and a half to two years to complete. If I did it all myself, it would probably take me four years to make one painting. My method allows me to work on several projects at once.

I draw on my own life experiences to create my work—sometimes even painful ones. In 1991 I married Ilona Staller, a Hungarian-born Italian porn star and politician. We had a son named Ludwig. Our union didn't last and in 1994, when Ludwig was eighteen months old, his mother abducted him from the United States and took him to Italy. A bitter custody battle ensued. For years I fought in the court system to get Ludwig back, but I was never able to. I was also prevented from interacting with him. It was one of the toughest times in my life. My world was turned upside down. My legal bills were exorbitant, and I lost everything in an effort to pay them. Everything. I even had to sell a lot of the art I had collected. I began to lose my faith in humanity and almost hit rock bottom, but at some point I realized that I had to hold on and rebuild my life. I wanted to be together for my son if things changed in the future.

Throughout this period, I constantly fantasized about a time when I would be on the other side of my ordeal and could celebrate. Consequently, I wanted to create art that would make life as positive and enjoyable as possible. I also wanted to create work that my son could understand. It was sort of my way of communicating with him from a distance. The result was *Celebration*, a series of large-scale sculptures and paintings of balloon dogs, Play-Doh, valentine hearts, and Easter eggs, among other things. Making these pieces really helped me through my trying time.

Something else that really helped me was being able to finally reconnect with Shannon in 1995. She had been adopted through Catholic Charities and they gave her information on her biological mother when she turned eighteen. Her biological mother then informed her that I was her father and that I had always wanted to raise her. Shannon made contact with me and came to New York with her adoptive mother to meet me. She then ended up going to Villanova University. Upon graduation, she moved in with me and stayed for several years. Eventually, she got married and created a wonderful family. We have remained very close.

Surviving such a tough time ultimately enabled me to become a stronger, better person. I became very involved with the International Centre for Missing and Exploited Children and created the Koons Family Institute on International Law and Policy, a think tank focused on the protection of children around the world. When you go through dark moments in life, it is important to remain optimistic. There is usually a way to make something positive out of a negative experience.

## JEFF'S PEARLS

■ Gaining recognition in the art world requires patience and a thick skin. Everybody encounters disappointments along the way. If even one person says, "I don't get it," about your work, it's easy to feel a real sense of failure. My work has been harshly criticized at times. When that occurs, I remember that not everything can appeal to everyone, and I brush it off and move on. It's essential to remember what your motives are and pull yourself together so you can be as fresh when you present your work to the next person as you were before the criticism. Nothing happens overnight, so to persevere you must enjoy the process and the journey.

■ It's a good idea for artists to inform the public of the intent of their artwork. I've never wanted to sit back and have a critic who doesn't even know me be the authority on what my work means and tell people from what perspective they should begin to look at it. Unfortunately, that ends up happening whether an artist likes it or not.

■ When I was a child, my parents got me a coffee-table book of Salvador Dali's work and I developed a real interest in him. He was very innovative and made a big impact on the art world. When I was in art school, I heard that he lived at the St. Regis Hotel in New York. I called him up, told him I was an art student who loved his work, and asked if we could meet. He said, "Sure." So I took the train in from Baltimore and we met in the lobby of his hotel. He was elaborately dressed in a fur coat, a silk tie with diamond pins, and a silver cane, and his moustache was twisted up at the ends. He invited me to see an exhibition he was having at a local gallery. We talked about his work, and he let me take some photos with him in front of one of his paintings. His generosity meant so much to me. Our encounter gave me the sense that if I wanted to do something I could. It's important for more established artists to be generous to younger ones. Whenever I am asked to visit a university or a school, I try my very best to make it happen.

# GARY HIRSHBERG
# STONYFIELD FARM CHAIRMAN AND CO-FOUNDER

**MY FATHER AND GRANDFATHER WERE SHOE MANUFACTURERS, AND THEIR
FACTORY WAS LOCATED ON THE BANKS OF THE SUNCOOK RIVER IN PITTSFIELD,**
New Hampshire. As a little kid, I loved to visit them at work. I would look out the windows
and watch the pretty colors from the dyes and chemicals flow out back and swirl around in
the river. To me, it was mesmerizingly beautiful. Only later did I realize that they were major
polluters. The Merrimack, into which the Suncook River emptied, was the tenth most pol-
luted river in the United States.

I witnessed my beautiful, clean, and rural New Hampshire change right before my eyes.
When I was young, we got our chickens and lamb from the next town over, our eggs from
down the street, and our milk delivered to our doorstep from neighboring farms. As the
years passed, these small family farms slowly disappeared. I also noticed changes in the
environment. Throughout my childhood, I was a ski racer and spent a lot of time in the
mountains. On a clear sunny day you could see the Atlantic Ocean from the top of Mount
Washington. By the early seventies, that view was gone. By the time I was sixteen, I had
realized that we were really screwing things up. I saw business and commerce as the source
of all things bad and became determined to undo the damage they had created.

I went to Hampshire College and I focused on environmental studies. I learned that we
were burying toxic waste everywhere, polluting and depleting water systems, and worsening

global warming (the resulting droughts, famines, floods, forest fires, and storms that we now take for granted are climate events resulting from putting too much heat and energy into the atmosphere). It became clear to me that if humans' egocentric behaviors persisted, subsequent generations would be prevented from having viable, healthy futures. We were endangering ourselves by disrespectfully trashing the only planet we'll ever have.

I also began to understand that we were changing the way food was made—for the worse. We were injecting our animals with hormones and antibiotics, spraying our fields and produce with toxic pesticides, and using chemical fertilizers, all with no real knowledge of what would happen to kids who grew up on a diet containing these things. I began to wonder if we were exacerbating the occurrence of cancer and other lethal diseases. Now we have scientific evidence that the chemicals in our food do indeed contribute to incidences of cancer. In addition, there is a direct correlation between pesticide usage and brain development— and even increased ADHD diagnoses.

I graduated in 1976 and wrangled an internship at the New Alchemy Institute, a non-profit research and education center dedicated to organic farming, aquaculture, and renewable energy. This eventually led to a full-time job as a water-pumping windmill specialist. I built many windmills, wrote a book on wind power, and edited another on organic farming. In 1980 I also started to lead ecological tours to China and worked as an environmental educator with the U.S. Fish and Wildlife Service.

But it was during Christmas of 1982, while visiting my mother, who worked at Disney's Epcot Center in Florida, that I had a life-changing epiphany. Kraft Foods had sponsored an exhibition called the Land Pavilion that showcased its vision of how produce would be grown in the future. Needless to say, their vision was very different from mine. The Land Pavilion demonstrated how food could be grown with rivers of chemical fertilizers, herbicides, and pesticides swirling past the naked roots of plants grown hydroponically in plastic tubes. This process may have produced food, but it was clear to me that this approach would lead to severe negative repercussions for both the environment and us.

The most startling thing I discovered, though, was that Epcot had 25,000 people paying to visit the exhibit every single day. That's more people than visited my New Alchemy Institute in an entire year—and that was free! Deeply disturbed, I blurted out to my mother, "I need to become Kraft Foods!" I still thought that their approach was flawed, but I realized that if I wanted to help prove that organic and sustainable food production could be every bit as viable, I had to stop resenting big businesses and harness such economic power to reach and influence large numbers of people. In order to transform the way that companies behaved, I needed to demonstrate that operating in an environmentally and socially responsible manner could be very profitable.

At the time, I was also a trustee of a little organic farming school in New Hampshire,

The Rural Education Center (TREC), run by my friend Samuel Kaymen. The goal of TREC was to help family farms survive and prosper, to keep food and food production healthy, and to help protect the environment. Samuel had a handful of cows and made delicious yogurt that he'd serve at our board meetings. He had enormous talents and strong principles, but handling the economic side of running a business was really not his passion. Plus, federal budget cuts had squeezed the amount of private philanthropic support that was available for efforts like this. As a result, TREC was in dire financial straits and virtually bankrupt. One day, the trustees and Samuel decided to try selling his yogurt locally to help fund the school. Samuel threw himself into the project and was able to borrow $35,000 from a group of Catholic nuns called the Sisters of Mercy to get things started.

Samuel and his wife, Louisa, named the yogurt business Stonyfield Farm and it launched in April of 1983. Samuel was phenomenal at making yogurt, but the business quickly got to be too complex for him to manage. Exhausted, he asked me to come on board full time and partner with him. The plan was that I would run TREC and help Samuel with the financial oversight while he would manage production and sales. Figuring that Stonyfield could be my "Kraft," I agreed to quit my other jobs and start in September. As soon as Samuel heard this news, he stopped paying any postponable bills, figuring that I would take care of such matters when I arrived. On my first day at work I discovered that we were more than $75,000 in debt and slipping further behind every day—and our electricity was about to get shut off.

So from the minute I got there I had to figure out how to raise money and get us out of our ditch. Initially, we thought $125,000 would cover us. We then realized we needed $200,000, then $500,000. As the business grew, I became more and more involved in operations on the farm. We were milking cows twice a day seven days a week, and during one especially difficult phase, every other night Samuel or I would have to stay awake to make yogurt. We were both perpetually on call and sleep deprived. It was a painful and often unhappy time.

Despite the hardships, we had a wonderful company and made an amazing product. However, garnering shelf space was a constant challenge. At that time, few Americans were eating yogurt and practically nobody knew what organic meant. When I talked to retailers to try to get them to carry Stonyfield, which was a little more expensive than the nonorganic brands, they'd say, "What does organic mean? Does it have dirt in it?" The few who did know what organic was thought it meant that you had to chew a little more. They associated it with heavy, doughy breads and dingy-looking broccoli.

In 1984, we exceeded our farm's capacity, so we decided to sell our cows and purchase milk elsewhere. Unfortunately, we couldn't find anyone to supply us with organic milk, so we focused instead on securing grass-fed, all-natural milk free of synthetic hormones and antibiotics. But we were not the only people out there attempting to sell an all-natural yogurt brand. When we started, Brown Cow, made in Ithaca, New York, had already been

in business for five years—so we also had to persuade those few retailers already familiar with natural products to carry our yogurt instead of theirs. We went to a Purity Supreme supermarket in Massachusetts the very same day that Brown Cow presented to them. Purity Supreme explained that they were going to carry only one all-natural yogurt and that it would be from whichever one of us gave them the best deal. Unfortunately, Brown Cow's terms were better than what we could afford to offer. Samuel and I sat in the parking lot after our meeting and decided that we had to go back in and match Brown Cow's terms anyway. It turned out to be one of the most pivotal decisions in the history of the company. Purity Supreme went with us because we were a local company, and before we knew it, Stop&Shop, Roche Bros., and other local grocery stores followed Purity Supreme's lead. With that one decision, we prevented Brown Cow from entering the New England grocery market, and thus eliminated our most serious competitor.

Because we couldn't afford advertising, we had to think up alternative ways to get to customers. Giving out free samples was our main method. For the first four years, we probably gave away about one cup of yogurt for every cup we sold. We constantly had to persuade people to taste it—but when they did, we frequently got them as a customer. We also discovered that amusing, outrageous behavior was a sure ticket to media coverage. One day, on Boston's number one radio morning talk show, the two hosts, Joe and Andy, mentioned Stonyfield. Joe suggested that Andy could get healthier by eating our yogurt. Andy replied that he would rather eat camel manure. While many businesses might see this as some kind of attack, we viewed it as an opportunity to strut our stuff. My wife, Meg, and I promptly drove to the nearby Benson's Wild Animal Farm where they had camels and filled a large yogurt container with camel manure. We showed up at the studios with noxious odors leaking out of the cup and offered Andy a choice of camel manure or our yogurt. Faced with the choice, he tried Stonyfield and admitted that it tasted better than camel manure. It was our first celebrity product endorsement and got us on-air mentions for about three months!

Despite us gaining some momentum here and there, making Stonyfield profitable was still very much an uphill battle. I produced dozens of business plans but none of them panned out. Something would always go wrong and set us back. For our first shipment to California, we hired a contract carrier to drive our yogurt across the country. As you can imagine, that was a big expense. Suddenly, the driver was out of touch and remained so for three days. No one had any idea where he was. Turns out he had parked his truck behind a Motel 6 in Nevada, went on a three-day bender, shot and killed a guy in a bar fight, and landed in jail. We had to fly someone out there to pick up the truck and finish the trip—a week late. Fortunately, it was winter, so even though the engine refrigerator had died, the yogurt was still cold!

In 1987 we partnered with an organic dairy in western Massachusetts. They had a factory with a lot of capacity, which we needed. We were in such a hurry to get into a new space that we weren't very diligent in assessing the fiscal condition of our new partner. About five months after we moved in, they went bankrupt. Suddenly faced with no production and a business doubling every three to four months, we had no choice but to bring everything back our original New Hampshire dairy. Our inefficiency there caused us to lose $25,000 a week for about fifteen months. And that was not money we had in the bank, so I had to constantly raise funds. It was a nightmare.

I would put on a suit, travel around to investor conferences, and try to borrow money or negotiate deals that would save us. A lot of people didn't want to invest because they thought our company would never work. Others had no interest in investing in something "weird" like yogurt. Many simply tried to take advantage of us. I got dozens of usurious offers from arrogant Wall Street guys. One of them even clipped his fingernails during our meeting! I was on a very steep learning curve, but I got to understand what was fair and what wasn't.

For every one person who invested with us, there were at least fifteen who turned us down—but we eventually wound up with 297 individual shareholders. Many of my family members invested. When my father-in-law died, he left Meg about $30,000 that I ended up borrowing to buy fruit, and my mother-in-law was actually one of our biggest investors.

For quite a few years, Meg and I lived on the farm in an apartment right next to Samuel and Louisa. Many nights, thinking Meg was asleep, I would tiptoe from our bedroom down the hall to my office and call her mother to see if she could lend us another $5,000 for payroll. I would often hear the click-click of call waiting. It was Meg on the other line saying, "Mom, don't do it!" It got to the point where my mother-in-law and I had secrets between us that we couldn't share with Meg because it was too stressful for her. Meg refers to that period as "the bad old days."

For many years, Stonyfield shareholders got a lot of yogurt and not much else. Most were quite patient, but some became very agitated and wanted out. Each year at Christmas, I would send everyone a note with the company news and I would write: "If you are interested in selling some or all of your stock, let me know." This ensured that no one felt trapped, but it also meant that I had to spend a big part of each year finding new shareholders to replace departing ones.

Samuel and I feared going under the whole time, but quitting and failing was never an option for me. There were several things that kept me going.

First, Samuel and I really believed in our mission and wanted to continue working for healthy food, healthy people, and a healthy planet. We *had* to succeed because if a company like ours couldn't make it, then what hope was there going to be for commerce to change paths?

Next, we got positive feedback—in the form of letters, phone calls, and visits—from people expressing how amazing Stonyfield yogurt was. I can't possibly emphasize enough

how much this encouraged us. An Iranian refugee once drove forty-five minutes to the farm just to tell us she had not eaten anything this good since she had escaped from Iran. And they've been making yogurt there for about one thousand years.

Most important, I was driven by a feeling of obligation to my investors. I had convinced these people to place their faith in me, and I was prepared to do everything humanly possible to not let them down.

For the first nine years, Stonyfield didn't make a nickel—but, finally, something shifted in the early nineties. Doctors started recommending that people eat organic, and when I went into supermarkets to talk to the buyers about organic food, they no longer looked puzzled. They actually needed the yogurt because consumers were demanding it.

Margaret Mead said, "Never doubt that a small group of thoughtful, committed citizens can change the world; indeed, it's the only thing that ever has." I have seen this happen first-hand with the organic industry. When consumers insist upon something, retailers provide it. When we purchase anything, we're voting for the kind of world we want.

In 1997 Stonyfield was able to pass Kraft in yogurt sales and in 2003 we bought Brown Cow. We are currently the world's largest organic yogurt maker and have also branched out into smoothies, soy yogurts, frozen yogurts, milk, and cream. We're still located in New Hampshire, but we now purchase our ingredients from a huge network of organic food producers. We've also maintained our devotion to planet-friendly business practices—from offsetting our emissions to making containers from plants instead of petroleum and generating our own renewable energy.

We have succeeded in proving that businesses don't have to choose between doing good and doing well—but the best reward for our persistence is that we've actually seen the world begin to change. Demand for organic food has won over the biggest names in retailing and every large manufacturer in the food space now has an organic product line. Plus, all the major food companies effusively describe their commitments to sustainability. While this may not always be 100 percent authentic, it certainly indicates that we've come a long way.


## GARY'S PEARLS

■  Think on your own and question authority. Authority is a short-lived phenomenon. It's who is in charge now, but that doesn't mean that they are right. So-called experts are often wrong. Also, just because something has been done one way for many years doesn't mean that it can't be altered. Challenging conventional wisdom can be scary, but most major changes happen because someone asked: "Why not do it differently?" If you don't ask, you don't get.

■ Don't compromise on the qualities that make your business unique. It's often tempting to do so because what makes you unique is frequently also costly—but the moment you're competing only on price, you've lost control of your venture. I'm not just referring to the attributes of your product; I'm also talking about the overall mission of your business. From the beginning, Samuel and I produced delicious and healthy yogurt. In hindsight, I realized everything that followed was made possible by our commitment to this. If we had lowered our price by using cheaper and lower-quality ingredients, we would just be one of many brands out there. Because we didn't, retailers had a reason to keep us on their shelf.

■ When you invest in an entrepreneurial venture, you're really investing in the people behind it. Take time to get to know their character. Look not at how they deal with success but at how they deal with adversity. When things are going well, everybody appears to be on top of their game. How they do when things are rough is the real question.

■ Determination is the most important ingredient for success. A superior product, a good business plan, creativity, and good instincts only get you on the game board. It all comes down to the moments when you either wave a white flag and give up or say, "I am going to keep fighting." The successful people are those who got back up after being knocked down, often repeatedly.

# CRAIG NEWMARK
# CRAIGSLIST FOUNDER

**MY HIGH SCHOOL YEARS HAD SOME PAIN ATTACHED TO THEM. I WAS THE CLICHÉ OF A NERD. I WAS INTO COMPUTER TECHNOLOGY, WORE THICK BLACK GLASSES THAT WERE** taped together, used plastic pocket protectors, and had the social skills that go with the stereotype. I didn't listen or articulate my ideas very well. I missed what other people found obvious. I just didn't get it—whatever *it* was.

I went to Case Western Reserve University where I got both my bachelor's and master's in computer science. During a communications class, I had an epiphany: It couldn't be everybody else who had a communication problem; it had to be me. This realization started me working on my communication skills. I still am.

After graduation, I had no real ambitions other than getting a job that was fun. Programming was fun, so I went with that. I worked at IBM for seventeen years. After IBM, I became an independent contractor, moved to California, and began developing web-oriented software for other companies. I worked for GM, Bank of America, and Charles Schwab. Unfortunately, most of the projects I worked on didn't pan out.

But one of the big advantages of Silicon Valley is that failure isn't stigmatized. It's assumed that most ventures will fail, so actually doing so is not that discouraging. The important thing is to keep trying. I've talked to a lot of people on the East Coast and in the UK and learned that in those places failure is stigmatized. I think that's why their business cultures have not been effective in some ways. Fear of failure can stop people from trying new things.

While I was writing software for companies, luck came along, and I stumbled on a new business while just trying to give people a hand. I noticed a lot of people using the Internet

to help one another out. Growing up as a nerd, I knew what it felt like to be left out. But rather than being bitter about that, I figured I should do something inclusive. So in early 1995 I started e-mailing all my friends about cool events going on in the Bay Area that usually involved arts and technology. The news of my e-mails spread and friends of friends wanted to be added to my list.

It wasn't long before people started suggesting that I branch out from just events. They asked me to post about jobs, stuff they had to sell, and apartment rentals. I listened to people's ideas and implemented the ones that made sense.

By the middle of 1995, my list had hit 240 addresses, too many to be sent by one e-mail. As a result, I decided to post it on a list server, which required a name. I wanted to call my list S-F Events, but friends suggested naming it Craig's List. They explained that this is what they all called it and that I should hold on to my brand. I didn't know what a brand was, but I adopted the name anyway. But with a lowercase c: craigslist.

Having no design skills, I kept the site very simple. I also figured that most people like things that quickly get to the point. I still believe that.

Being a nerd, I'm pretty literal. If I say I am going to do something, I follow through. So I kept running craigslist as a hobby for a few years. By the end of 1997, I was getting about a million page views a month. It became a lot for me to deal with on my own, so I brought on some volunteers to help out. Unfortunately, that wasn't too successful. In 1999 I realized that I needed to get serious. I decided to devote myself to craigslist full time, hire some really smart people, and incorporate it into a company.

I think it's important to know when to get out of your own way. I suck as a manager. Luckily, I was aware enough to hire and promote a guy named Jim Buckmaster in time for craigslist to become what it is. I'm the chairman and founder, but Jim runs the company. Thanks to his presence, I've had time to launch craigconnects.org to help connect the world for the common good. I'm also active outside of my online comfort zone, working on issues for veterans and military families and others in need and also serving as a board member or advisor to a number of nonprofits.

Despite the fact that craigslist has become a serious business, it's also remained a serious community service. We're a simple platform where people can help one another with everyday needs. I believe we've endured because we've remained loyal to our roots. Our motto is "Give people a break." We treat our users the way we would like to be treated and have worked hard to form a culture of trust. For me, this translates into a strong focus on customer service, which led to craigconnects and my other activities outside of craigslist. However, even today I continue to engage in craigslist customer service every day to stay connected with our community. We've continued to listen to suggestions from our users and act on them. Whenever we make decisions, we think about what's good for the community. Although somewhat unusual in the business world, this way of operating feels right to us and has worked.

Every now and then, people come along and want to convince us to change the focus on community service that has led to our success and focus instead on short-term profits. I believe that this would be a mistake because our success as a company has been driven by our attention to what the community wants and needs. We are committed to this principle as our North Star to guide our way in the future.

People have sometimes asked me why (unlike many other founders of successful companies) I'm not interested in doing the usual Silicon Valley thing and becoming wildly wealthy. My answer is that once you've been able to make a comfortable living and prepare for your future, what's the point in making more and more? I know some of the richest people in Silicon Valley and all that money doesn't make them happier.

## CRAIG'S PEARL

■ Brevity is the soul of wit. If you've got something to say, say it and stop talking. If you don't have anything to say, you're doing yourself and others a favor by keeping quiet. If you can't make a contribution, don't slow down the people who can. Most of my life I've probably been unaware of when to stop talking. I try to adhere to these rules, but not with complete success.

# STACEY SNIDER
## CO-CHAIRMAN, 20TH CENTURY FOX

**ALTHOUGH MY MOTHER DIED WHEN I WAS ONLY NINETEEN, SHE WAS THE GREATEST INFLUENCE ON MY LIFE. I AM WHO I AM BECAUSE OF HER. MY MOM HAD MY SISTER AND** me in her early twenties and was divorced by the time she was twenty-nine. Instead of going to a traditional college, she went to art school and, as a result, relied primarily on my father for financial support.

Wanting her daughters to end up in a better position than she was in, my mother emphasized the importance of education and nurtured our feminist identities. She took us to march for women's rights, gave us the book *Our Bodies, Ourselves* (a progressive book about women's health and sexuality), and continually admonished us to make our own way in the world. I became a diligent student and, having grown up in Philadelphia, decided to attend the University of Pennsylvania for my undergraduate education. My dad and grandfather were lawyers, so law school seemed like the next logical step. I wanted to stay close to home and go to Penn Law but got rejected so, in 1982, I enrolled at UCLA instead. Little did I know how much that rejection would alter the course of my life.

I enjoyed law school, but the actual practice of law turned out to be a completely different story. I have always been happy to work and feel most connected to who I am when I'm busy and productive. I waitressed throughout college, and while in law school, I wrote coverage (synopses of screenplays for film production companies) for fifty dollars a shot. During summers between law school, I went for the stereotypical jobs: I clerked for a federal district court judge and interned for both a big Manhattan litigation firm and a boutique firm in LA. It was at these summer jobs that I felt something completely new—a kind of malaise, ennui,

and impatience with my workday. The emotions were so uncharacteristic that they scared me into serious self-exploration.

I went to one of my former college professors for advice. He instructed me to write down what I love and said we would figure out a way to make a career out of that. Growing up, I always had my nose in a book, to the point of compulsion (even now, if I have five or ten minutes and I'm not reading something, I feel anxious), so I wrote down "reading." I said to him, "How am I going to make a living doing that?" My professor explained that I was already doing just that by evaluating screenplays and that I should think about what the next step along that path might be. I realized that if I became an agent I could work with writers. I figured that my legal background would not only help me protect and make great deals for my future clients, but it would also help me to get my foot in the door at an agency.

I reasoned that if there was ever a time for me to be bold and try something exciting it was right then. Having never made real money, I was still used to being at the bottom of the ladder financially. First-year salaries at law firms were higher than anything I could have imagined. I knew that if I went that route I would get used to the money, adjust my lifestyle accordingly, and perhaps get trapped.

Despite my Ivy League education and a law degree, the best job I could get was in the mailroom of Triad Artists, an LA-based talent agency. Checking my ego at the door, I spent my days photocopying scripts, pushing a mail cart around the office delivering mail to the agents' desks, and doing various package runs, one of which involved picking up fifty thousand dollars' worth of chains for Mr. T. I was once sent to deliver a script to Steven Spielberg. All I did was push the button and hand the script to the person who met me at the gate, but I remember thinking, *Wow! I'm in show biz!*

After about five months, I got promoted to the position of assistant in Triad's talent department, which is basically just another way of saying "secretary." My duties now included placing phone calls, making dinner reservations, picking up dry cleaning, and driving the agents' spouses to premieres. I was also given a variety of seemingly impossible tasks. For example, my boss once said, "Find Marlon Brando in Tahiti. I need to talk to him." Another time I had to go out in the middle of the night and deal with an agent who was about to be arrested for a DUI. I somehow had the presence of mind to ask the cop to give her a field sobriety test instead of a Breathalyzer test. I figured the agent's adrenaline might kick in and give her a shot at passing the field sobriety test, which is exactly what happened and she avoided jail.

Working in an entry-level agency position definitely separates the wheat from the chaff. Those with a positive attitude gulped and thought, *I have no idea how I am going to do this, but I will.* Others either felt indignant that the things we were asked to do were ridiculous or they panicked at the challenges and quit. Now and then I'd feel sorry for myself and think, *How can I have all this education yet be spending my days doing this?* But the next day I would realize what an idiotic attitude that was, and I would resolve to take advantage of the situation and learn as much as I could.

Only years later did I realize how much I got out of that period of my life. An entry-level job at an agency is almost like taking an extra year of graduate school. It's like a survey course of the entertainment business. You get an overview of all the different areas and players: film, television, digital, actors, writers, producers, agents, and executives. The variety of assignments thrown at you forces you to be resilient, to think on your feet, to fine-tune your powers of persuasion, and to manage different personalities. One of the biggest lessons I learned during that time was that when you deal with someone it's advantageous to know as much as you can about them. We all had to memorize the client list and know exactly what everyone did. I still research new people I am going to meet. I also made some great long-standing friendships. There was a certain gallows humor among those of us who stuck it out. We would lean on one another and lend a helping hand whenever we could. Without a doubt, all these things aided me in my career down the road. An entry-level position at an agency is now the job that I recommend to people who are interested in the entertainment industry. As a matter of fact, it's precisely the job my eldest daughter had the summer before her senior year of high school.

While working at Triad, I learned that representing artists was one step removed from what I really wanted to do: help writers bring their ideas to the screen. I set my sights on becoming a studio executive (studios finance and supervise a broad slate of films then market and distribute the finished product) and I went to work as a secretary at a film production company called Simpson-Bruckheimer.

In 1986, following one of my periodic self-pitying moments at Simpson-Bruckheimer, I got a burst of energy and called a friend who was working as an assistant to a literary agent in New York. I said, "You have to help me. I am withering on this vine and need to make something happen. Is there anything you've come across that could be interesting to make into a film?" She told me about a book by a first-time author that she thought had the makings of a great courtroom thriller. It turned out to be *Presumed Innocent* by Scott Turrow (which went on to become a huge best seller). I begged her to send me the manuscript and she did. I actually remember waiting in the parking lot for the Federal Express truck to arrive, that's how excited I was. I made the rookie mistake of getting my boss, Don Simpson, all hyped about the book before I'd even read it, but I got lucky because it was a real page-turner. Don wanted to adapt *Presumed Innocent* into a film, but he got outbid for the rights in the end. However, because I was responsible for first bringing *Presumed Innocent* to LA, my name got mentioned amid all the buzz, and a day or two later I was recruited to be director of development at the production company Guber-Peters. In my new position I would be responsible for soliciting new material for the company, recommending which scripts should

be developed into movies, and working with the writers to make this happen. It was what I had been striving for. I jumped at the opportunity.

While working at Guber-Peters, I realized how helpful my law school education was. The critical thinking that I had developed there enabled me to distill almost any issue down to its essence and understand exactly what has to happen for a problem to be solved. This, combined with everything I learned as an assistant, proved to be a good blend, and I was able to slowly but steadily move up the ranks. After a few years, I was running Guber-Peters and assisted on *Batman*, *Rain Man*, and *Single White Female*, among many other films. Shortly thereafter, in 1991, Sony needed a head of production at TriStar, one of its other movie labels, and I was offered the job. Much to everyone's dismay, I turned it down.

In Hollywood there are two kinds of executives: The flames that burn brightly and quickly go out and the executives who have long, interesting, and powerful careers. I aspired to be one of the latter. Being successful in one's position is the only way to have a long and secure career. If you bite off more than you can chew, it feels great in the moment, but then what? I turned down the job as head of production at TriStar because I didn't feel that I had the experience necessary to do it well.

The position went to an executive named Marc Platt. Once he was in place, I joined TriStar and worked for him. He was a great mentor and friend. In 1995 Marc left TriStar and I got promoted to his position. At that point, I was ready. During my tenure there we made *Jerry Maguire*, *Sleepless in Seattle*, *As Good as It Gets*, *Legends of the Fall*, and *Philadelphia*, and they were nominated for many awards. It was a wonderful time and I even had my first child in the midst of it all.

In 1997 I was recruited to be head of production at Universal and accepted the job. Although the move was a lateral one, the company was bigger and had more resources. I continued as head of production until 1999 when my boss, Ron Meyer, offered me the position of chairman of Universal. At this point, my second daughter had just been born. I hesitated to accept the promotion because of the huge responsibility it would entail, but Ron cautioned me, "Sometimes the timing isn't perfect—and you might not be asked to this party again." That made me pause. I discussed it with my husband, a wonderful fifty-fifty partner, and after making sure Ron and I saw eye to eye about what I required as a working parent, I said yes.

Being chairman of Universal was a seven-day-a-week job, but I felt I could handle it. Parenting young kids is physically demanding, but I was able to take my daughters along on business trips because they were not in school yet. As they got older, however, they needed me in different ways. My responsibilities became more difficult to juggle and balance, and I began to feel that I was missing time with them that I would later regret. During my tenure at Universal, we put out the *Bourne* series, the *American Pie* series, the *Meet the Parents* series, *Erin Brockovich*, *A Beautiful Mind*, and *Brokeback Mountain*, among other films—but as well as things were going, the demands of my job became impossible to justify.

When my contract came up for renewal in 2006, I did not extend it. Instead, I joined DreamWorks as CEO and cochair. It was a smaller company, and without the corporate and travel duties I had at Universal, I could be with the kids every night and on weekends.

I have always viewed my career as a rolling wave. While I do think that both men and women can "have it all," I don't think anyone can have it all at once. You need to figure out what your priorities are and then fulfill your potential at each stage of your life. I love my work, but family is forever, and that's what really sustains me. I've seen close friends, and many other women, wait to get pregnant then not be able to. It's devastating. On one hand, women have been urged to focus on their careers and not feel rushed, but on the other hand, there's science and biology, which are nonnegotiable.

It's important to approach the personal aspects of life with as much urgency as we do our careers. When you decide it's time to have children, do it. Men don't ask their boss's permission; they assume they are entitled. My advice also extends to finding a life partner. You can passively hope that cupid shoots his arrow at you or you can be proactive. In my early thirties, after having been divorced, I let those around me know that I wanted to meet someone great. My husband and I were fixed up by a colleague of mine. If I hadn't specifically told her that I was looking, she would probably not have thought to introduce us. If you are purposeful and can articulate your goals, whatever they may be, you have a much better chance of achieving them.

## STACEY'S PEARLS

■ People say that if you can do what you love you're very lucky. My advice is to put yourself in a position to discover what you love. Many students are so focused on getting the right grades so they can get into the right school that it barely gives them the chance to try something zany. I wasn't wired that much differently, but I always tried to zig a little bit when everyone else zagged so that I could have the possibility of surprise in my life. When most of my peers took the usual "check the box" classes at Penn, I took Russian history and discovered that I had a passion for history. It's no coincidence that a lot of the movies I've worked on (*Lincoln, Gladiator, A Beautiful Mind*) have involved historical figures. If I hadn't allowed myself to venture off the beaten track, I wouldn't have discovered an enthusiasm for something unexpected.

■ It's important to be able to present your ideas well, especially in writing. Unlike a face-to-face conversation, something in writing can be endlessly reviewed to make sure that your ideas are presented exactly the way you want them to be. I often rely on this skill when the subject matter I'm discussing is sensitive and I really need to modulate my tone.

■ I read an article in the *New Yorker* by the neuroscientist Robert Sapolsky that rocked my world. Sapolsky, who listened to only the music he grew up with, had a young research assistant who came into the office and listened to a completely different genre of music every day. Sapolsky was irritated by his assistant's open-mindedness, mainly because it made him focus on his own narrowness. Being a scientist, he was prompted to study the subject and came to the conclusion that as we age we become less and less open to new things.

While many people love the comfort of having familiar ground underfoot—"This is what I listen to." "These are the five restaurants that I go to."—businesses rarely evolve that way. In order to keep up in my field, for example, I need to be open to new experiences: new music, new television shows, new actors, and new trends. Luckily, I've always been pretty receptive to novelty, but reading Sapolsky's article has made me be more purposeful about it.

■ Movies are at their best when they either faithfully represent a culture or when they are aspirational. Either way, storytellers need to make sure that when women appear onscreen they are presented with as many complexities as they actually possess. As far as we've come, there are still, unfortunately, not enough movies about substantive women. In my position I try to make a difference. For example, DreamWorks decided to make the movie *The Help*, which had been turned down by every other studio because all the main characters were women. I understood that a lot of guys probably wouldn't be interested in seeing it, but that doesn't mean it shouldn't be made. It means it shouldn't be made for any budget. We also made *Lincoln*. It would have been easy to make it all about Abe, but we made sure to remember his wife, Mary Todd, and the important role she played in his life.

■ I hate getting the rug pulled out from under me. As a result, I always try to anticipate what might go wrong in any situation. I think this stems from the shock and sadness I felt from my parents' divorce, which seemed to come out of nowhere, but serves me well professionally. I like to work in a transparent environment and always encourage people to give me the bad news and not sugarcoat anything. You can always find data points that suggest success, but it's important to pay attention to those that suggest a problem. This way you can make improvements.

# HELENE GAYLE
## CARE USA PRESIDENT AND CEO

**I GREW UP IN A WORKING-CLASS FAMILY IN BUFFALO, NEW YORK. MY PARENTS WERE PEOPLE OF STRONG FAITH—NOT IN A DOGMATIC WAY, BUT THEY FELT DEEPLY THAT** part of living one's faith was to think about others first and give back to society.

After church on Sundays, my father would take my four siblings and me to visit some of the elderly people in our community. Sometimes we would bring them food, and other times we would just socialize. My mother, a social worker, used to tell us, "If somebody makes a reasonable request, your answer should always be yes." My parents also put a high premium on education. My siblings and I were expected to attend college and then have a profession. I realized early on that I wanted to use my education as a way to give back.

I pursued medicine, thinking that it was a practical tool to help people, but the career path I ultimately took was defined, at least in part, by the commencement speech at my younger brother's college graduation. The speaker was D. A. Henderson, dean of the Johns Hopkins School of Public Health and one of the leaders of the international effort to eradicate smallpox. He spoke about how they were able to wipe smallpox off the face of the earth by using the tools of public health. I was in medical school at the time and had vaguely considered going into public health, but D. A. Henderson crystallized it for me. Public health is practicing medicine at the population level instead of at the individual level. I realized that in this field I could use my skills as a doctor to have a positive impact on large groups of people—even on the world.

So, during medical school, I also got a master's degree in public health. Afterward, I completed my residency in pediatrics and then went to the Centers for Disease Control and

Prevention (CDC) in Atlanta for a two-year training program in epidemiology, which is the study of how disease spreads and the ways it can be controlled. I originally planned to stay only through the end of the program, but I fell in love with the place and ended up staying twenty years. I held various positions at the CDC, but my main focus was combating HIV/AIDS. When I started in 1984, HIV was very new. My colleagues believed that it would remain confined to pockets of marginalized people in our society and wouldn't become an important public health issue, so they counseled me against focusing on that "strange" disease. Little did anyone know that it would become one of the defining public health issues of our time.

In 2001 I was offered a job directing the HIV, TB, and Reproductive Health Program at the Bill and Melinda Gates Foundation in Seattle. Leaving the CDC and moving across the country was both a personal and professional risk. At the CDC I had risen through the ranks to one of the most senior positions. Although the Gates Foundation is now one of the largest, most important foundations in the world, back then it was still developing and was relatively unknown. Some friends and colleagues advised me against it but, intrigued by the opportunity to try something different, I took the job. The transition was a lot harder than I expected. I didn't have any friends in Seattle, and after two decades working in a large governmental organization, I found the free-flowing culture at the privately funded Gates Foundation foreign. For the first six months I kept thinking, *Maybe I should just call the CDC and ask if I can have my job back.*

But I had made a commitment and decided to tough it out, which was definitely the right choice. During my time with the Gates Foundation, I got to observe how one builds an organization from the ground up (I started out as the only employee in my division, and it now has a couple of hundred people) and I developed a better understanding of privately funded philanthropic establishments and their ability to foster positive social change. My experience there equipped me to be a better candidate for my next job.

After five years at the Gates Foundation, I was offered and accepted a job as president and CEO of CARE USA, a global humanitarian organization whose main goal is to eradicate poverty. The transition from the medical and health field into the broad arena of global development was a major one. Once again, colleagues advised me not to make the move. They questioned why I would want to give up the security of being an expert in my field and thought I would regret leaving a position at a foundation (where I dispensed money to those in need) for a job where I had to raise money. But I saw moving to CARE as a chance to broaden my work. In my new role I would be able to address some of the underlying social and economic factors that fuel health inequities and keep people trapped in poverty. I could potentially have an even greater impact on preventing death and disease than by using only health interventions.

I want to make as big a difference in the world as I possibly can. In order to achieve this goal, I continually expose myself to new arenas where I can potentially learn something useful. Doing this enables you to grow, but even as you push past your comfort zones, it is easy to be riddled with self-doubt. For instance, I recently had the honor of being asked to sit on the boards of both Colgate-Palmolive and Coca-Cola. At meetings I am predominantly surrounded by people who have decades of experience in business and are at ease with a world that is fairly unfamiliar to me. To live up to my responsibilities as a board member, I've had to learn about corporate finance and other core business issues. It's been challenging but absolutely worth it. I've gained a better understanding of the corporate world, which is important for our work at CARE, where we are increasingly developing partnerships with businesses.

When people make career moves that don't appear to take them on the most linear, expected path, there are often detractors out there saying it's a bad idea. I am practical and certainly explore the positives and negatives of every situation, but in the end my decisions result from following my passion. You can't map your life out with any precision and you have to get comfortable with that. You must also be willing to take risks and be deliberate about seizing opportunities that are off the beaten path. If you are curious about life and explore new things, you'll continue to expand your options.

For many years I routinely found myself in situations where I was the only "whatever" in the group—whether it was the only person of color, the only woman, or the only person younger than forty. Walking into a room filled with people who are different from you can be intimidating. It's also easy to be underestimated in those scenarios. I know there have been times when people have shown a lack of confidence in me and assumed I was not up to the task at hand. When this happens, I become even more motivated to show people that I am where I am because I have the necessary skills and ability.

Understanding how you are being stereotyped is the first step in remedying it. There have been times, for example, when I've realized that someone was not treating me as an equal because I am a woman. Feeling like a victim leads to victim behavior. Addressing an issue restores your power. On more than one occasion I have tactfully expressed to a male counterpart that I think he would be treating me differently if I were a man. Another way to cope with being discriminated against is to build networks of mentors and people who support and believe in you. Don't be afraid to turn to these people if you feel undermined. They can help you build yourself back up.

Life is an obstacle course comprised of things that knock you down completely as well as the smaller day-to-day struggles. When I encounter tough times, personally or professionally, I get through them by remembering my core beliefs. I want to use my remaining time on this earth in ways that are meaningful to me. Thinking about the approximately eighty million poverty-stricken people CARE reaches each year always motivates me to persevere.

## HELENE'S PEARLS

■  Social change is better achieved by being for something than against something. Growing up, I was part of a protest generation. We protested the war and stood in support of liberation struggles in Africa. Whenever we saw a problem, we were "against" it. It's easy to think that by being against something you're standing up for a cause, but if you want to have a greater impact, you need to ask yourself, "What do I stand for and what do I want to happen?"

■  The human potential and the power of the human spirit are unlimited. I have seen people start out with a two-dollar loan and end up becoming professionals who sent all of their children to college. While there are realistic limitations for everybody, if you set your mind to something, you can achieve most of what you want in life.

# HANS ZIMMER
## COMPOSER

**I GREW UP IN MUNICH, GERMANY. MY MOTHER WAS VERY MUSICAL AND ATTACHED TO OLD WORLD TRADITION. SHE TOOK ME TO MY FIRST OPERA WHEN I WAS ABOUT THREE,** then dragged me to classical concerts at least once a week until I was about twelve, at which point I rebelled. All I wanted to do was listen to loud rock and roll.

My father was a successful engineer and inventor who was ahead of his time and not afraid to try new things. He came up with all sorts of crazy inventions, some of which actually panned out. He died when I was six. My mother was devastated and filled with worry as to how we were going to get by. I wanted to put a smile on her face and remember thinking, *I'll play the piano!* We lived far away from any other kids and didn't have a television—so I carried on playing the piano and took great refuge in it.

It wasn't long before I stopped playing the classics my mother wanted me to play and began to modify the piano any way I could. I wanted to figure out how to make new sounds. I know my father would have thought my experimentation was fantastic, but it made my mother gasp in horror.

The prevalent view in Germany at that time was that if you didn't follow the rules and do well in school you wouldn't amount to anything. Looking out for my best interest, my parents and teachers tried to get me to conform, but I was beyond salvage from the start. It wasn't that I was a bad child; I just couldn't stop my mind from wandering. When on occasion I did tune in, I would interrupt and question everything. My grades, of course, were terrible. If anything came after an F, that's what I should have received. A teacher once threw a chair at me in music class. I was kicked out of nine schools and wound up at a boarding

school in England. I was continually told that I would end up in prison. As a last resort, my mom sent me to a typing class.

What I loved—and did in all my spare time—was make music. On account of my father's profession, I was introduced to computers at a very young age and embraced them as musical instruments. I also began playing keyboards and synthesizers as a teenager. My lack of formal music education didn't matter (I did once take two weeks of piano lessons, but I quit because I didn't like the structure). The technology was just being invented so everyone had to make things up as they went along.

I remained in England after boarding school where I played in seedy clubs and dives with a few pop bands—the most well-known being the Buggles, who sang "Video Killed the Radio Star." In the meantime, I did other music-related gigs. I composed jingles for commercials and music for BBC miniseries, and I was known as the Synth Wiz because of my skills at programming that instrument.

Making a lot of money has never motivated me—and for many years I had hardly any. Similar to my experience with schools, I often found myself getting chucked out of apartments for not paying the rent. It wasn't deliberate, however—the truly important, existential things never quite filtered through my daydreams. On one hand, being a poor artist sucked, but in many ways it was a grand life. I was surrounded by other poor artists. At the end of the day we would all sit around a table, have interesting conversations, then suddenly pick up our instruments and make music together. That created a feeling I couldn't find anywhere else. Days went into nights, and nights went into mornings. The only time we noticed that we didn't have money was when the electricity would get turned off.

Eventually, I took a job as assistant to the composer Stanley Myers. We scored a few films together (including *My Beautiful Laundrette*) then decided to start our own recording studio. We worked on fusing music from traditional instruments with electronic instruments. The first film I was hired to do alone was called *A World Apart*. The director Barry Levinson later got a hold of that soundtrack and hired me to score his film *Rain Man*, my first Hollywood job and a real turning point in my career.

I had imagined that Hollywood was going to be technologically far ahead of anything I'd seen in Europe, but when I arrived, I found it to be quite the opposite. Composers there were not yet using computers, which made the dialogue between them and the director very cumbersome. The composer would play his tune on the piano and have to say something like "This is where the French horns come in." The director had to imagine what that would sound like. The first time a director could actually hear the music would be when a full orchestra was assembled. What if he didn't like it? Making changes was a lot harder. I, on the other hand, composed the *Rain Man* score on my computer in Barry Levinson's office. He loved that he could listen to my work as it was forming. Instead of making him imagine what the French horns would sound like, I'd bring them in on the computer.

*Rain Man* went on to win the Oscar for Best Picture and earned me my first Academy Award nomination. This led to jobs on an increasing number of high-profile films such as *Thelma & Louise* and *Driving Miss Daisy*, among others.

The people behind *The Lion King* heard some of my music and offered me the job, which I took for all the wrong reasons. The other movies I had worked on were not geared toward children. I now had a six-year-old daughter and wanted to show off by taking her to the premiere of a film that I had scored. What surprised me was that I really got into the story— which is about a son losing his father. Because I lost my father at a very young age, I was able to tap into a profound and honest part of myself. It was the first time I expressed serious emotions through music. I ended up winning an Academy Award, a Golden Globe, and two Grammys for *The Lion King*. You never know what can come from a humble children's movie if you approach it honestly and genuinely.

Music is a huge part of the tone of a film, but my job isn't to do precisely what directors ask. If they knew exactly what they wanted, they would do it themselves. My job is to create something that they can't imagine: a parallel story expressing what's not already present in words and images. By the time a film is handed to me, everyone else has done all they can to make it as good as possible. Inevitably, some parts don't live up to what people imagined so, because I'm the last in line, they're all hoping I'll be able to fill in whatever is lacking. Although I am always incredibly excited when someone comes to me with a job, I also always feel a tremendous sense of responsibility and pressure right from the start.

Having people love what you do is seductive. Like most artists, I know how to repeat something that's been a success, but if I start just regurgitating what I've done before, I'm not growing. The only way I can maintain this life is to go directly against that temptation and create new things. I feel very fortunate to keep getting work, but because I've done so much, I have an underlying fear that I have nothing left in the drawer. I've got twelve notes to work with—and every other composer is using those same twelve notes. I wonder, *What's going to make what I do so different from what everybody else does?"* I become terrified that I will let everybody down, including myself.

The first step in the process is to understand the movie's story. It doesn't take long for a possible framework to start sparking in my head, but translating that into a tune is agonizing. Sometimes it takes me two or three weeks of just sitting in my studio—sixteen, seventeen, eighteen hours a day not coming up with anything. I get obsessive and can even work myself into a panic. Don't invite me to a dinner party. I'll probably forget to show. I'll say, "See you at seven o'clock," but then at ten to seven an idea will pop into my head. I'll think it will only take me two minutes, but the next time I look at my watch it's two in the morning. It's not that I forgot about the dinner party; it's that real life doesn't even exist. Of course,

this trait has been a problem in my marriage, but let's not even start that discussion! When I'm in a real panic, I literally don't go home for the weekend.

Part of the problem is that I'm a perfectionist. Even when the tune is complete, there's often a little critic sitting on my shoulder saying, "It's no good. It's no good." It's not uncommon for me to continue working on something until the director or producer comes to me and says, "The movie has to come out. Give me whatever you've done right now." Even at that point I fight tooth and nail for more time. I know every trick in the book and have a thousand excuses as to why it's not ready or why I may even need to start over again. I drive people crazy, of course—myself most of all.

I was hired to do the score for the film *The Dark Knight*. On the last day of recording with a one-hundred-person orchestra, I found myself lying on the couch in the back of the room experiencing terrible chest pains. I hadn't slept in weeks and was thinking, *I'm going to die*. But I didn't say anything. Chris Nolan, the director, who knows me very well, saw that I was in serious trouble. He walked over to the microphone and announced to the musicians, "I think we've recorded enough. You can all go home." I sat up and said, "No, no, no, no! We haven't!" Chris repeated, "I think we've recorded enough." And, of course, he was right.

After all these years, I have come to realize that I must go through a period of agony and torture before I have a breakthrough. My big ideas frequently come at the very last moment, when a deadline is beating me up like crazy. I think we all have some fear of failure in us, and it's a great motivator. Sometimes, however, I really do have to accept defeat. I'll realize that something I've been working on for weeks isn't good and I will chuck it out. I used to feel terrible when this happened and I resisted getting rid of anything—but I have come to realize that it's part of the creative process and now I am prepared for it.

## HANS'S PEARLS

■ If you look at the downside of any vocation, you can find a million reasons not to pursue it. But if you try to play it safe and pick a career because you think you should, it most likely won't end well. Whenever I need legal or medical advice, I stand up in front of my orchestra and announce my problem. Half of the musicians are doctors and the other half are lawyers whose parents forced them into those jobs.

■ People used to tell me to find a *real* job. Hearing this worried me deeply, but not enough to give up music because I was so passionate about it. At one point somebody (I believe it was James L. Brooks) told me that it's okay to do the thing you love. That sort of freed me up to relax into what I do. I still check with myself every morning and ask, "Do I want to go to the studio and write music?" To this day, it's the most exciting thing I can think of doing.

■ My music has often been ahead of its time and, as a result, easy to criticize. When I was a teenager, hearing people cut down work I was proud of was very painful. But as time progressed, the feedback went from my mother's neighbors complaining about the "ungodly noise" I was making to them asking, "When is your son coming back to play some of that beautiful music again?" The main difference was their perception. I was basically playing the same thing.

■ Your worst qualities can also be your best, so try to utilize them in a positive way. In my case, the characteristics that got me thrown out of school ended up making me successful in my career. Music-related thoughts are always whizzing around my head, and I compose through daydreaming and questioning things. I'm also very stubborn, which has been a huge advantage because I stick with things when others might not.

■ It's essential to work with people you feel safe being completely candid with. When I was scoring *The Power of One*, the director first wanted the music to be similar to what's in the film *Out of Africa*, with big, lush orchestras. I suggested we do the whole thing with Zulu choirs instead, which he eventually thought was a good idea. I started working with a couple of choirs in Los Angeles—but no matter what I did it kept sounding like gospel music. I used up the entire budget but was still not happy with the outcome. I finally went to the producer and said, "I have to admit defeat. Let's just scrap my Zulu idea and I'll write the nice orchestral score that the director originally requested." The producer said, "The only mistake you are making is that you're not in Africa." That was on a Thursday. By Monday morning I was in a township in South Africa, in a warehouse with two microphones and this incredible choir rocking the roof. It was amazing.

■ Creative people should try to do something new every day. Whether it ends up being good or bad doesn't matter. What's important is to keep your muscles exercised. You've got to practice a lot before you can be any good at most things. The majority of skilled musicians I know have been practicing about eight hours a day from the time they were six or seven years old. I played all day long and still do. One of the reasons I continue to work so much is that when I've taken any lengthy break I feel rusty when I return. I imagine it to be the way a runner trains every day. If he stops for any period of time, his muscles atrophy and he'll have to work even harder to build them up again.

■ Take the time to know your technology. I see many musicians completely relying on recording engineers and producers because they are not up to speed on the current tools. I think, *This is your baby and you are letting other people do all that stuff to it?* The last thing you want to do is to be at the mercy of someone else.

# DANIEL BOULUD
## CHEF

**I WAS BORN AND RAISED ON MY FAMILY'S FARM OUTSIDE OF LYON, FRANCE. WE NEVER REALLY TRAVELED, BUT WHEN I WAS ELEVEN, MY PARENTS TOOK ME TO BRITTANY,** a region in the northwest corner of the country. Friends there invited us to a restaurant on the coast, and we ordered a *plateau de fruits de mer*. I had never seen anything like it. It was three layers with about ten different kinds of seafood. There were baby gray shrimp, small pink shrimp, and langoustine. There were oysters, littleneck clams, large clams, and razor clams alongside crab and lobster. It was majestic. In that moment, I realized that traveling to experience new kinds of food is one of the most beautiful things you can do. After that, whenever I went on a trip, the journey was always for food—to eat something unique, something special, something delicious. You can see churches and other sights, but the best souvenir for me is always my memory of the food.

I decided I wanted to become a chef. When I was fourteen, I got accepted to a three-year apprentice program. It was similar to a hotel school, but it was for young people who wanted to be chefs. The program was in Lyon, so I moved there and lived in a spare room at my uncle's place. I worked twelve to sixteen hours a day—splitting my time between school and a very good restaurant in town. While my friends were off playing soccer and skiing on weekends, I worked. It was trying, but I learned so much: how to shop for food, peel every type of vegetable, fillet every fish, and pluck every game bird.

Most mornings, while picking up supplies at the local market, I would see a chef named Paul Bocuse. If there had been a gang of chefs in Lyon, Paul would have been the leader. Although he lived in a small town, this man was respected, admired, and in demand all over

the world. He traveled a lot and made the rest of us dream about places like the United States, South America, Australia, and Asia. To me, being able to travel and have people appreciate your talent all over the world was the quintessential reason to be a chef. (Today, Paul is eighty-eight and, in my opinion, no other chef has had a greater impact on the industry. He is basically the Dalai Lama, or the pope, of cooking.)

Two years into my program, when I was sixteen, I had a big fight with the restaurant's head chef. When it got physical, I ran out of the kitchen and into the dining room to protect myself. The restaurant's owner, who liked me very much, said, "Don't touch this kid! Leave him alone!" Rather than lose his job, the chef left me alone—but he got me back a year later. When I graduated from the program, I took an exam and scored in the top five out of about 170 young cooks. This made me eligible to enter a national competition to determine who was the best culinary apprentice in France, which I thought would be a great launching point for my career. But to do so, I needed to be registered by a mentor. The chef I fought with (my only prospect to register me) refused. He wanted to destroy my career. Although I was already motivated to succeed, this made me even more so. I wanted my vengeance. I wanted to become better than he was. When someone tries to get in your way, don't let it squash your ambition or stop you, just change course and keep going.

I went on to work at a few different restaurants in France and did some catering on the side. Slowly climbing my way up the ladder, I was trained by some of the country's most renowned chefs. I paid close attention to the way they conducted themselves. I wanted to know what made them so distinguished and figure out how to get there. Not only did I hone all of my cooking skills, but I also learned a great deal about managing a kitchen and providing good customer service.

When I was twenty-one, my boss offered me an opportunity to be a sous chef (the chef ranked just below the head chef) at his restaurant in Denmark. It was a big promotion and my first chance to indulge my work-travel fantasy. I loved it. In 1980, when I was twenty-five, I got an offer to go to Washington, D.C., and work as a private chef for an ambassador at the European Commission. I took it, of course.

I think that up until the age of twenty-eight or thirty, people should try to learn and experience as much as they can. If you don't really know what you want to do, work for high-quality successful people in different fields. If you know what you want to do, take a variety of jobs within that field. For example, if you want to be a chef, work in a restaurant with a staff of fifteen then one with a staff of 120 to see the different organizational scale. Experience different cuisines whenever you can, try new restaurants on your days off, and immerse yourself in the world of food. Every one of my jobs and experiences taught me something about the restaurant business. Diversification broadens your foundation and makes you better equipped for whatever the future brings.

After three years in Washington, D.C., my diplomatic visa ran out. In order to stay in America, I had to find an employer to sponsor me. The search was harder than I expected, but I finally found somebody willing to hire me as a sous chef for a restaurant he was planning. Six months later, as the restaurant was about to open, I realized that I hated the management, the chef, and the food. Although I had no other job leads and was panicked about possibly being forced out of the country, I told my bosses that I'd help them open the restaurant but then I had to leave. Before surrendering and going back to Europe, I decided to ask a friend, the chef Jean-Louis Palladin, for help. He telephoned a friend who was opening a restaurant at the Westbury Hotel in New York. I went in for an interview and got the job. When you feel like you've lost your compass, it's okay to ask for directions.

I remained at the Westbury Hotel for two years then went on to open a restaurant at the Hotel Plaza Athénée, where I stayed for another two years. Then, in 1986, I made a life-changing career move: I was hired as the executive chef at New York's Le Cirque. During my six-year tenure there, Le Cirque became one of the most highly rated restaurants in the country. This brought me a lot of confidence and enabled me to build a very strong reputation as a chef.

In 1992, I left Le Cirque with the hope of opening my first restaurant. I had no money of my own to invest, but I knew that I had talent and wanted to find the right partners. I wanted them to be honest and have an understanding of finance and business that I didn't. I dreamed big and wanted to raise $2.5 million. My good friend Lili Lynton introduced me to her uncle, Joel Smilow, who was about to retire from his position as the chairman and CEO of Playtex Products. Joel said, "I would like to be the only investor and want to back you up 100 percent. It will be much easier to work together if it's just the two of us, and I think we'll do very well." Joel's trust and confidence made me feel that all the sacrifices I had made over the years were paying off. We opened our restaurant, Daniel, in 1993 on Manhattan's Upper East Side and have never looked back. Shortly afterward, Daniel received a coveted four-star rating in the *New York Times* and three stars in the New York City Michelin Guide. In 1994, we started a catering business called Feast & Fêtes and have since opened two retail establish-ments and five restaurants in New York City, two in Florida, and one in each of the following cities: Singapore, London, Toronto, Montreal, Las Vegas, Washington, D.C., and Boston.

Although we have done extremely well, not every restaurant we've opened has been a success. For example, we opened a restaurant in Vancouver in 2008. We went there because the owner, who was very persuasive, had lost his chef and thought that bringing me on board would be the best thing for them. We did what we could to make everything work, but it was the wrong location and the wrong partner. We spent a lot of time, energy, and money trying to build something we shouldn't have, and it was very frustrating. But I try to learn from mistakes and move on. When you get kicked off your horse, the important thing is to get back on and ride with pride.

The restaurant business depends on good teamwork. My staff, from the dishwashers to the pastry cooks to the waiters and the maitre d's, is my greatest asset—and much of my success is linked to the fact that many of them have been loyal and remained with me. It's important to incentivize your employees and reward them for what they do. We try to compensate everyone properly and give them a real opportunity to succeed. When someone with talent sticks with us, they get promoted. About seventy-five percent of the openings we get for executives are given to people who have grown up with me professionally. The executive chef at Daniel, for example, has been with me for seventeen years and has worked his way through every position in the group to get to where he is. Treat your employees with respect, and they will remain an asset. Treat them as expendable, and you will have difficulty holding your team together.

We put a tremendous emphasis on making our customers happy, but on occasion, people come in with such a chip on their shoulder that there is nothing anyone can do about it. This, unfortunately, happens in all service-oriented businesses. In the early days of Daniel, I didn't always handle this type of situation well. One woman was so abusive to my staff and me from the moment she sat down that I literally pulled her chair out and said, "Please get out of here. No one's going to cook for you. No one's going to serve you." I'm much more experienced and mellow now! If you encounter miserable customers, don't take it personally—instead, view it as a challenge. Remember that your job is to serve politely and professionally, and make people feel special. If you don't have a very good reason to bother with an issue, let it go. (Complaints, by the way, are not always unfounded. They are right as often as they are wrong, and they can help you improve and make corrections. It is important to be attentive to criticism and learn from it.)

Working in the restaurant world demands a huge amount of sacrifice. When others are getting together and having fun—Christmas, Easter, Fourth of July, Mother's Day, Thanksgiving—you are working. You also work long hours on regular days, so it is difficult to have much of a personal life. If you choose this profession, stop comparing yourself to others. The restaurant world is another planet. You have to make a choice and not look back.

Restaurants are my passion and consume my thoughts. Anyone who can find this kind of excitement in life is lucky. You may work till you are bone tired, but you won't mind because there's nothing else that you would rather be doing. And your ambition will carry you from one milestone to another.

## DANIEL'S PEARLS

■  No matter what business you are in, remain focused on what you like and become very knowledgeable about it. If Ralph Lauren, for example, had been all over the place with his designs, he never would have been able to build what he has. Instead, he focused on something very specific and did it well. You have to have your mantra. For me, it's French cuisine and being French. If you are in a creative field, know the heritage you are inspired by. I have French cookbooks that go back to the 1600s and 1700s. They are difficult to read, but seeing what chefs were doing back then is fascinating and initiates creativity in me. Although I am inventive with my cooking and have many different influences, everything is practiced within the parameters of French cuisine.

■  It's important to find good mentors. To get this opportunity, if you want to be a chef, try to get your foot in the door of the best restaurant you can—one that maintains a good reputation year in and year out. (This shows that the people there can not only cook, but that they can also manage a business well.) These jobs are competitive and you may have to start as an intern, but it is an opportunity to learn and network.

■  Many businesses are built on connections. Don't take any relationship for granted (you never know where your coworkers will end up down the road) and always leave each job on a good note. Throughout my career, I went above and beyond what was expected of me. In turn, my bosses respected me and wanted the best for me. Every new job I got was with the help of the chef I had been working with. A good reference from your previous employers is essential.

■  You don't have to be in a big city like New York or Los Angeles to be a successful chef. If you cook well and create the right environment, the public will find its way to you. You can become the superstar of a much smaller city.

# FRANK GEHRY
# ARCHITECT

**MY HIGH SCHOOL HAD A SHELF OF BOOKS DEDICATED TO VOCATIONAL GUIDANCE. I REMEMBER LOOKING THROUGH THE ONE ON ARCHITECTURE AND THINKING IT SEEMED** so bloody boring. My cousin was a chemical engineer and one of the most successful people in my near family, so I decided I should become one too. My school arranged for me to spend a day with a chemical engineer at his lab. But at the end of the day, the guy looked at me and said, "Frank, you didn't get excited about anything. This profession is not for you." I thought, *Okay, so I won't be a chemical engineer.*

My father sold and serviced slot machines. He was uneducated and, although street-smart, never made much money. He had a lot of stress in his life and would often take it out on me. He used to tell me that I was a useless dreamer with no business sense and that I wouldn't amount to much. My mother compared me to her friends' children and always thought I fell short. But I knew I was curious and had ambition. I was drawn to people who were on the intellectual side, and my friends were interested in things like classical music, literature, art, and politics.

During my senior year of high school, my father had a heart attack and was unable to work, so he lost what little business he had. He became wiped out financially and totally demoralized. We were living in Canada at the time and my parents decided we should move to Los Angeles, where we had some family. That's what sick people were being advised to do back then—go to warmer climates and start over. With no real skill set to fall back on, my father became a truck driver for a soda pop company. My mother worked at a department store. I pitched in by becoming a truck driver for a breakfast nook-furniture company and by

doing other odd jobs on the side—like washing airplanes and working at my cousin's jewelry store. We all did what we needed to do to survive.

I attended night classes at Los Angeles City College because they were free. I had always enjoyed art and loved to draw as a child, so I decided to take a drafting class. The teacher thought I had some aptitude for it, but I didn't find it interesting. I tried a class on perspective drawing instead and failed it. I was so upset about the F that I took the class again and got an A.

One of my cousins was a student at the University of Southern California (USC) and kept pushing me to enroll there. My family couldn't afford anything like that, but I managed to get a job in the USC admissions office, which allowed me to take a few classes through their extension program. I took a night class in ceramics and the teacher, Glen Lukens, liked me so much that he asked me to be his teaching assistant. We became close. Glen happened to be building himself a house by Raphael Soriano, a big-deal architect in Southern California at the time. Although I still had no idea what I wanted to do in terms of a career, Glen had a hunch that I might enjoy architecture so he took me to the construction site when Soriano was there. I remember watching him—this little Greek guy with a broken nose dressed entirely in black with a beret—directing the workers to move the steel and other materials. He really knew what he was doing and it was exciting. Glen saw my eyes light up and enrolled me in a USC night class in architecture.

I got an A and the teacher recommended that I enroll in the USC School of Architecture—and skip right to the second year of the program! It was the first time I had received positive reinforcement of that magnitude and it felt great. It was a really big deal for me. I applied for scholarships and worked on the side. While at USC, I got married. My wife, Anita, worked as a secretary to help pay my tuition.

Halfway through my second year, one of my professors called me into his office and said, "You will never make it in this field. Get out now or you're just going to waste a lot of time." Hearing this was devastating, but at the same time something allowed me not to take it personally. My professor's comments felt like anti-Semitism to me, something I had gotten used to while growing up in Canada. (My family was one of approximately thirty Jewish families in our town—Timmins, Ontario—and for a while, I was the only Jewish kid at my school. I used to get beat up regularly for "killing Christ.") Also, I had become so enamored with architecture that it would have been almost impossible for anyone to derail me. I had reached the point of no return and vowed to prove that professor wrong.

I graduated with a bachelor of architecture degree from USC in 1954 and began working for the LA-based architect Victor Gruen, whom I had apprenticed for while in school. Within a few months, however, I got drafted and served in the army for about two years. The army encouraged people to go back to school and would let you out three months early if you did, so I decided to apply to graduate school. I wanted to use architecture to do good things for the world, so I applied to a city-planning program at the Harvard Graduate School of Design and got accepted. But when I got there, I discovered the program was nothing like what I had expected it to be. It was about economics, government, and statistics—not architecture—so I quit. I was on the hook for a year of tuition, so I stayed for that time period, but I was allowed to enroll in any class I wanted.

Afterward, I moved back to LA and resumed working for Victor Gruen. I was given a lot of responsibility and learned how to do everything from building shopping centers to writing contracts and budgeting. It was an incredible experience, and it really boosted my confidence, but Anita wanted to live in Paris. I started saving money and, after about three years, we finally made the move (we had two daughters by this point). It was difficult to find employment, but I managed to get a job working for a French architect four days a week. The rest of the week, we would travel around looking at architecture. I loved France, but I barely made enough money to get by. It wasn't terrible compared to what other people in this world go through, but we had to miss a few meals so the kids could be fed, and we lived in a basement apartment. After about a year, as we were preparing to move back to LA, Victor Gruen came to Paris and asked to meet. He was going to open an office there, and he wanted me to join him. For a split second, I was excited by the prospect of being able to stay and afford a better life, but within one minute, I said no. It was a risky move for someone with a family to support and no game plan, but somewhere along the way, I had become determined to open my own practice and figured I should start then.

When I returned to LA, a friend told me that his in-laws were planning to build a little warehouse there and he felt I would be a good fit for the job. He offered me $2,000 to do it and I accepted. I got a couple of other projects from that (apartment buildings and houses) but my career wasn't progressing the way I had hoped. Projects would fall through and I couldn't understand why. I was on the verge of bankruptcy and, to top it off, my marriage had run into serious trouble and I was having difficulty with my two daughters. Basically, I was floundering on all fronts.

A friend pushed me into therapy with a man named Milton Wexler, and I joined a fifteen-person therapy group that Milton led. We met twice a week, and I went for two years without saying a word. I would literally just sit there in silence. Then one night Milton turned to me and said, "Your anger is showing." This opened up the floodgates and the entire group came at me. They wanted to know who I thought I was, sitting there judging them. If it had been only one or two people criticizing me, I could have shrugged it off, but when a group attacks, you can't ignore it. That was powerful stuff. I had no idea I was exuding my anger, but once I knew that it was being read, I became motivated to do something about it.

Milton and I explored the issue further, and I realized that my anger was getting in my

way professionally. I would often decide beforehand that a prospective client wouldn't get me, and I would walk away from potentially good opportunities. In addition, projects weren't working out because people were uncomfortable with me. Building something new and original can be scary because no one wants to push it too far and end up with a structure people make fun of—so it is essential for clients to trust their architect. Understanding all this was a major turning point. It enabled me to dismantle the wall I had built around myself and connect more with people. As a result, my career progressed, and I was able to move toward larger projects. (I still fall back into my old patterns from time to time, but at least I am aware of it and try not to.)

Milton guided me through other issues too. My profession has all these rules about what fits and what doesn't. The kind of buildings I was designing didn't conform to any particular architectural philosophy, and many of my colleagues were dismissive of me and made fun of my work. When I would discuss this with Milton, he would say, "Screw them! There aren't any rules. Just because they did it that way last week doesn't mean you have to do it that way today."

The artists in town accepted me and gave me positive feedback—so I became friends with them. Observing the way they worked really influenced me. When an architect draws up a plan, he has to go through many, many people to get whatever it is built. Artists, on the other hand, have a more direct process and can be more freewheeling. They are also not wed to tradition and history. They have no rules. I was drawn to this freedom.

In 1975, I got remarried to my current wife, Berta. A couple of years later, we bought a pink bungalow in Santa Monica that was built in the 1920s and needed work. We didn't have a big budget, but I was excited to finally be able to do whatever I wanted, however I wanted. The house became my architectural laboratory, and I experimented with industrial materials such as chain-link fence, corrugated aluminum, and raw plywood. I decided to leave the old house intact and basically build a new one around it. The finished product was quite unconventional and really stood out (especially since it was the only two-story residence on the street and was located on a corner). My neighbors hated it, but many felt otherwise and it garnered a lot of attention.

Although I had evolved and become secure with my own style, I also needed to make a living, and I felt that I had to take on various jobs that were out of whack with what I believed in for that purpose. This all changed one evening.

At the same time that I was doing my house, I was also building a shopping mall called Santa Monica Place for one of my largest clients, The Rouse Company. The night Santa Monica Place opened, Matt DeVito, the president of Rouse came to my house for dinner. He looked around and said, "What the hell is this? You must like this house, since you did it for yourself. But if you like this, how can you like Santa Monica Place?" I explained that I didn't.

Matt's response was that I shouldn't take on work I didn't want to do. At that time, about forty-five people in my office were working on various Rouse Company projects, but Matt and I shook hands and agreed to stop working together. That was a Friday. I went into my office on Monday morning and let nearly everyone go. It was like jumping off a cliff—scary, but exhilarating at the same time.

In a way, that turning point was similar to both my decision to decline Victor Gruen's offer in Paris and my decision to quit Harvard's city-planning program. It was tough rebuilding my practice after parting ways with The Rouse Company (I had to work day and night to stay afloat) but there are times when you know that you need to believe in yourself, be bold, and not go forward with something that doesn't feel right. I still turn down work for this reason. Once in a while, I regret doing so, but you can't always be correct.

In the late 1980s, I was chosen to do the Walt Disney Concert Hall in downtown LA. This was a huge project for me, and I was ecstatic. It ended up taking fifteen years to complete and was on the verge of not being built several times, but that's life in this field! In the meantime, in 1991, I got a job that changed my career. I was hired to design the Guggenheim's new museum in Bilbao, Spain. It opened in 1996 and had a tremendously positive impact on Bilbao. The museum paid for itself within the first eight months of opening, and it now attracts about one million visitors a year. It transformed what was once a gritty industrial city in economic decline into a vibrant one, and it has become an immense source of pride for the city's inhabitants. What happened to Bilbao has become known as the "Bilbao effect" and other cities have been attempting to emulate it. (When I was working on the museum, by the way, I had no idea that it would receive the reaction it did. I remember people talking about their hopes that it would result in a commercial uplift for the city. I thought that was like believing in the tooth fairy!)

Since Bilbao, clients who hire my firm generally aspire to do something unique. They know what I am about and egg me on to explore. It's really exciting, but whenever someone comes to me with a new project, I'm always a little scared that I won't know what to do. It seems like most creative people live with this kind of insecurity. It's actually healthy because it helps the creative process and leads you to new places. If you don't have it, you probably ain't gonna measure up. But in the end, you have to trust your intuition and be willing to take risks. Risks allow for progress—and this applies to all fields.

I've taught architecture for many years and love doing so. One of the most essential messages I try to get across to my students is the importance of finding your own language. When I was at USC, I was inspired by Frank Lloyd Wright—and some of my early work looks creepily like his—but as soon as I realized what I was doing, I cleansed myself and stopped. I tell my students to take out a piece of paper and sign their names, because everyone's signature has a different aesthetic. I say, "That's yours. You did it intuitively and that's what

you've got to do in other areas of your life. Don't look over your shoulder at what other people are doing. When you are yourself, your work will be stronger and you will slowly realize that you are the only expert on it—so what other people say won't matter."

My work gets criticized all the time and it can get pretty harsh. If I am criticized because I inadvertently did something that hurts somebody, I pay attention. Otherwise, I just do the best I can and keep moving forward. If people like what I create, I'm thrilled. If they don't, I don't try to sell them on it. You can't please everybody.

## FRANK'S PEARLS

■ Question everything. Curiosity is the lifeblood of creativity. Growing up as a Jew, I studied the Talmud, which continually poses questions. This was the foundation for my way of thinking. I continually ask, "Why do we have to do it that way? Can't it be done this way?" This trait has been critical to my work.

■ You will be judged on everything you do. It doesn't matter what field you are in: If you are working on something large or something small, always make sure it adheres to your highest standards. Move away from people who dilute this mission and partner with those who support it.

■ Anger management is a serious and prevalent issue. I see so many people in various professions who should have made it but have fallen by the wayside because they weren't able to control their anger. I want to catch them and say, "Stop!" If you can look in the mirror and realize your anger, you can help yourself. If you are not sure, ask a friend, "Am I angry?" If so, figure out why and work to get rid of it. If you decide to see a shrink, finding the right one for you is essential. I'd been to a few before Milton, but none of them understood me the way he did.

# ACKNOWLEDGMENTS

I am grateful to so many people for making this book possible—it took a city!

Thank you to everyone who helped me brainstorm, scheme, and connect with prospective subjects: Ruthie Abel, Bill Ackman, Charles Baker, Craig Balsam, Alex Barnow, Samantha Bass, Susan MacTavish Best, Sara Blakely, David Blau, Jan Bohrer, Ruma Bose, Joe Brenner, Sarah Brokaw, Cara Buono, Elizabeth Burke, Christy Callahan, Jennifer Rogers Carlock, Lisa Chajet, Lyor Cohen, Rodney Cohen, Steve Cohen, Laurie Crain, Liz Delorme, David Ebersman, Meredith Elson, Billy Etkin, Elisabeth Familian, Rebecca Feuerstein, Erin and Jon Frankel, Chris Gartin, Scott Glass, John Glickman, Wendy Glickman, Tony Godsick, Becky Goldring, Gary Goldring, Julie Grau, Gordon Greenberg, Scott Greenberg, Marni and Bruce Gutkin, Richard Halvorson, Jenny Harris, Ellen Bronfman Hauptman and Andrew Hauptman, Betsy Hayes, Steve and Caren Holzman, Riva Horwitz, Robert Kaplan, Margaret Riley King, Dan Klores, Dr. Albert Knapp, Tom Kuhn, Emily Kuriloff, Mark Kurlansky, Dave Larson, Lena Leitman, Steve Levine, Alex Lloyd, Wendy and Steve Master, Johnny McCormick, Tod Mercy, Cliff Michaels, Darcy Miller, Alan Mnuchin, Michael Oates Palmer, Cynthia Park, Joanna and Moses Port, Emily Prins, Jessica Queller, JJ Ramberg, Cornelia Reiner, Jenny Reinhardt, Adam Schefter, Tom Scott, Roy Sekoff, Jill Sherman, Jonathan Marc Sherman, Brian Siberell, Chris Silberman, Matt Sirovich, Edward Skyler, Lesley and Tommy Slatkin, Larry Smith, Robyn Sorid, Nick Spencer, Pat Steel, Jill Swid, Peter Thum, Rachel Tore, Wendi Trilling, Josh Uffberg, David Weinreb, Amanda Beasley and Nicky Weinstock, and Jonathan Weisgal and his cousin, Jonathan Weisgall. And to my youthful sounding boards: Shade Ashani, Elizabeth Crowder, and Bronte Hughes.

Thank you to Allison Burnett, for giving me invaluable feedback on practically every aspect of this book from the time it was conceived. You are so talented and always get "it" faster than anyone else. As you know, I've been hooked since high school!

Thank you to Orin Snyder, an amazing friend and an incredible lawyer. I am deeply appreciative of your continuous support and I am awed by your triple backflips.

Thank you, Charles Lu, for your loyalty, reliability, and for your expert help with my photos.

Thank you to my agent, Andrew Wylie. You are the definition of a class act and I am beyond lucky to have you on my team.

Thank you to my editor at Abrams, Eric Himmel, for believing in *Getting There*, and to Sarah Massey for your outstanding editorial assistance. You have both been a pleasure to work with.

Thank you to my family: To my extraordinary mother, Leanor Segal, for continuously cheering me on and for being there for me on every front. To my brothers and sisters-in-law, Andrew, Raquel, Justin, Jennie, Zachary, and Dara Segal, for your help with this book and for your support in general. And to Sage, for the patience and understanding you showed when I was busy working on this book, for your genuine interest in every subject's story, and for coming on four of the interviews/photo shoots with me!

Rob Fraley, thank you for *always* making yourself available to obsess over every detail of this book with me, for your very constructive feedback, and for your unwavering love and encouragement.

Finally, THANK YOU to all of my subjects for agreeing to participate in *Getting There*! Without your wise insights and candid narratives, this book would not exist. I admire each and every one of you—and quote you often!

Editor: Sarah Massey
Designer: Strick&Williams
Production Manager: Anet Sirna-Bruder
Library of Congress Control Number: 2014942734

ISBN: 978-1-4197-1570-9

Printed and bound in the United States
10 9 8 7 6 5 4 3 2

Abrams Image books are available at special discounts when purchased in quantity for premiums
and promotions as well as fundraising or educational use. Special editions can also be created to
specification. For details, contact specialsales@abramsbooks.com or the address below.

THE ART OF BOOKS SINCE 1949

115 West 18th Street
New York, NY 10011
www.abramsbooks.com